THE
MAYA

Michael D. Coe

Penguin Books

Penguin Books Ltd, Harmondsworth,
Middlesex, England
Penguin Books, 625 Madison Avenue,
New York, New York 10022, U.S.A.
Penguin Books Australia Ltd, Ringwood,
Victoria, Australia
Penguin Books Canada Ltd, 2801 John Street,
Markham, Ontario, Canada L3R 1B4
Penguin Books (N.Z.) Ltd, 182–190 Wairau Road,
Auckland 10, New Zealand

First published as a volume in the 'Ancient Peoples and Places'
series, edited by Glyn Daniel, by Thames & Hudson 1966
Published in Pelican Books 1971
Reprinted 1972, 1973, 1975, 1976, 1977, 1980

Made and printed in Great Britain by
Richard Clay (The Chaucer Press) Ltd,
Bungay, Suffolk
Set in Monotype Bembo

PELICAN BOOKS

The Maya

Born in New York City, Michael Coe studied
English literature and anthropology at Harvard
College, and took a doctorate in anthropology at
Harvard University under Professor Gordon Willey
in 1959. He taught at the University of Tennessee,
moving to Yale University in 1960, where he is now
Professor of Anthropology. He is also Adviser to the
Robert Woods Bliss Collection of Pre-Columbian
Art, Dumbarton Oaks, Washington, D.C.

Dr Coe, who has excavated in Mexico, British
Honduras, Guatemala, Costa Rica, and Tennessee, in
1966 began, with the support of the National Science
Foundation, a long-term field project among Olmec
sites in Veracruz, Mexico.

Among his previous published books are *Mexico*
(1962), *The Jaguar's Children: Pre-Classical Central
Mexico* (1965) and *America's First Civilization:
Discovering the Olmec* (1968).

Contents

Illustrations

Plates

Figures

Foreword

Ancient Mesoamerica, defined as the civilized portions of pre-Conquest Mexico and Central America, is a subject so large and complex that it could not be handled properly in a text of this length. Accordingly, it was decided to divide it between two volumes, of which the first, covering only the non-Maya peoples of Mexico, has already appeared. The present book consequently deals with the Maya themselves.

Probably more study has been devoted to these remarkable people than to any other in the aboriginal New World. In degree of cultural development, they were head-and-shoulders above the rest of the American Indians of the hemisphere, and have for nearly a century and a half continued to excite the interest of scholars and laymen. Many general books, some of high merit, have been written on the Maya. But within the past decade some quite remarkable advances have been made towards understanding what this civilization was really like. What was its social and political order, what the nature of its 'cities' and settlements; what subject matter is dealt with in the hieroglyphic texts; on what economic base did Maya civilization rest; and what is the background from which Maya culture sprang? These are questions for which we now have at least partial answers, and this book is an attempt to view the ancient Maya in the light of these findings, although it is realized that there is still much to be learned.

The emphasis will be upon Maya civilization in the Classic

Period, especially in the region where it reached the greatest florescence: the lowland forests of northern Guatemala and near-by states of the Republic of Mexico. But this achievement will be placed in its proper historical and geographical context, for the high point of Classic Maya culture was not reached in isolation, nor did the Maya invent everything with which they have been credited.

A few words should be said about the pronunciation of Maya names and words. The system of orthography comes to us from the early Spanish friars who were attempting to record the native language of Yucatán, so that most vowels and consonants are as in Spanish. However, the good monks were plagued by the fact that many Maya sounds were unknown to Europe and so had to devise new ways of writing them down. The letter *x* is used, as in sixteenth-century Spanish, to record a phoneme like English *sh*; *c* is hard, no matter which vowel follows it; *u* before *a*, *e*, *i*, and *o* is pronounced like English *w*. The Maya languages make an important distinction between glottalized and non-glottalized consonants, the former being enunciated with constricted throat. In the revised orthography of Yucatec Maya these would be as follows:

Non-glottalized	Glottalized
c	k
ch	ch'
tz	dz
p	pp
t	th

Glottal constrictions or stops may also occur between reduplicated vowels, although these are ignored in most dictionaries. In general, the accent or stress is on the last syllable of a word.

It is a pleasure to record my gratitude for the aid which I

received in the writing of this book. Once again, I am indebted to Dr Glyn Daniel and Dr Geoffrey Bushnell for all the encouragement I received from them. From my colleague Professor Floyd Lounsbury I have received the benefit of his own yet unpublished research into Maya writing and social structure. The maps and some of the drawings are by Mrs Jean Zallinger and Mr Peter Zallinger. Finally, thanks go to all of those who have generously provided photographs used in the plates.

CHRONOLOGICAL TABLE

DATES	PERIODS	SOUTHERN AREA		CENTRAL AREA	NORTHERN AREA
		Pacific Coast	Highlands		
1530	Late Post-Classic		Mixco Viejo	Tayasal ↑	Independent States Mayapan
1200	Early Post-Classic	Tohil Plumbate	Ayampuc	(abandonment)	Toltec-Maya
900	Late Classic		Amatle-Pamplona	Tepeu	Puuc, Chenes
600	Early Classic	Cotzumal-huapa ↑	Esperanza	Tzakol	Regional Styles Acanceh
300 / 150	Proto-Classic		Aurora Santa Clara	Matzanel	
A.D. / B.C.	Late Formative	El Baúl Crucero	Miraflores	Chicanel	Late Formative
300	Middle Formative	Conchas	Las Charcas	Mamom	Middle Formative
800				Xe	Maní Cenot
	Early Formative	Cuadros / Ocós	Arévalo		
1500	(Archaic)				

[1] Introduction

The Maya are hardly a vanished people, for they number an estimated two million souls, the largest single block of American Indians north of Peru. Most of them have resisted with remarkable tenacity the encroachments of Spanish American civilization. Besides their numbers and cultural integrity, they are remarkable for an extraordinary cohesion. Unlike other more scattered tribes within Mexico and Central America, the Maya are confined with one exception to a single, unbroken area that includes all of the Yucatán Peninsula, Guatemala, British Honduras, parts of the Mexican states of Tabasco and Chiapas, and the western portions of Honduras and El Salvador. Such homogeneity in the midst of a miscellany of tongues and peoples testifies on the one hand to a lack of interest on the part of the ancient Maya in military expansion, and on the other to their relative security from invasions by other native groups.

There are few parts of the world where there is such a good 'fit' between language and culture: a line drawn around the Maya-speaking peoples would contain all those remains assigned to the ancient Maya civilization. It would be an error, though, to think of these peoples as existing in some kind of vacuum. In pre-Spanish times they belonged to the larger grouping christened 'Mesoamerica' (figure 1) by Professor Kirchhoff. The northern frontier coincided approximately with the limits of aboriginal farming in Mexico, the desiccated plateau beyond holding out only the possibility of humble collecting and hunting. To the south-east, the Mesoamerican border ran from the Caribbean to the Pacific across what is now Honduras and El Salvador, dividing the civilized Maya from simpler peoples of foreign tongue.

All of the Mesoamerican Indians shared a number of traits which were more or less peculiar to them and absent elsewhere in the New World: hieroglyphic writing, books of bark paper or deerskin which were folded like screens, a complex permutation calendar, a game played with a rubber ball in a special court, highly specialized markets in which chocolate beans were used as money, an emphasis upon self-sacrifice and mutilation, and a pantheon which included a rain god as well as a culture hero known as the Feathered Serpent. Also in all Mesoamerican religions was the idea of a multitiered heaven and underworld, and of a universe oriented to the four directions with specified colours (figure 40) and gods assigned to the cardinal points and to the centre.

The ancient triad of maize, beans, and squash formed then, as it still does, the basis of the Mesoamerican diet, but of course these foods were widely spread elsewhere, from the south-western United States to Peru and Argentina in pre-Conquest times, wherever native cultures had advanced beyond a level of semi-nomadic simplicity. In Mesoamerica, none the less, the preparation of maize is highly distinctive: the hard, ripe kernels are soaked or boiled in a mixture of water and white lime, producing a sort of hominy which is then ground into unleavened dough on a quern (*metate*) with a handstone (*mano*) (figure 36) later to be fashioned into steamed *tamales* or into the flat cakes called *tortillas*. The latter are characteristically toasted on a clay griddle which rests upon a three-stone hearth.

From such profound similarities one can only conclude that all the Mesoamerican peoples must have shared in a common cultural origin, so far back in time that it may never be brought to light by archaeology. It is also reasonable to assume that there must have been active interchange of ideas and things among the Mesoamericans over many centuries, which in itself would tend to bring about cultural homogeneity. It was out of such a matrix that Maya civilization was born.

The Setting

There can be few parts of the globe as geographically diverse as Mesoamerica, which includes almost every ecological extreme from the snow-swept wastes of the high volcanoes to parched deserts and to rain-drenched jungle. The Maya area is situated in the south-eastern corner of this topsy-turvy land, but actually is somewhat less varied than the larger unit of which it is a part. For instance, high-altitude tundra is not found, and deserts are confined to narrow stretches along the upper Río Negro and middle Río Motagua. It is also true that tropical forest is more extensive here than in Mexico outside the Maya area.

There are really two natural settings in the land of the Maya: highlands and lowlands (figure 1). In geology, in animal and plant life, and in the form that human cultures took, these are well set off from each other. The Maya highlands by definition lie above 1,000 feet and are dominated by a great backbone of volcanoes (plate 2) both extinct and active, some over 13,000 feet in altitude, which curves down from south-eastern Chiapas towards lower Central America. This mighty cordillera has been formed principally by massive explosions of pumice and ash of Tertiary and Pleistocene age which have built up a mantle many hundreds of feet thick, overlain by a thin cover of rich soil. Millennia of rain and erosion have produced a highly dissected landscape, with deep ravines

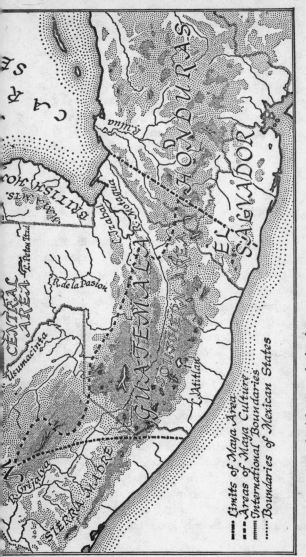

Figure 1. Major topographical features and cultural areas

between hog-back ridges, but there are a few relatively broader valleys, such as those of Guatemala City, Quetzaltenango, and Comitán, which have long been important centres of Maya life. Not all of the highlands are so recent in origin, however, for to the north of the volcanic cordillera is a band of more ancient igneous and metamorphic rocks, and beyond this a zone of Tertiary and Cretaceous lime-stones which in the more humid country bordering the lowlands take the fantastically eroded appearance of a Chinese landscape. Isolated to the north-east are the Maya Mountains, a formation of similar antiquity.

Highland rainfall is dependent, as in the rest of the New World tropics to the north of the Equator, upon a well-defined rainy season which lasts from May through early November. In effect, this follows a double-peaked distribution in both highlands and lowlands, with heaviest falls in June and in October. For the highlands, the highest figures are registered along the Pacific slopes of Chiapas and Guatemala, a zone noted in pre-Conquest days for its cacao production, but in general the total precipitation for the Maya highlands is no greater than for the temperate countries of northern Europe.

The highland flora is closely related to soils and topography; on the tops of slopes and ridges, pines and grasses dominate, while further down in ravines where there is more moisture, oaks flourish. Compared to that of the lowlands, the wild fauna is not especially abundant, but this may be due to a far denser human occupation.

Native farming practices in the highlands are quite different from those of the lowlands, although inhabitants of both regions depend upon the burning of unwanted vegetation and upon rest periods for farm plots. The moderate fallowing practised in the highlands depends upon the position of the field on the slope, with only about ten years of continuous cultivation possible in higher fields, after which the plot must be abandoned for as much as fifteen years, while further down up to fifteen years' continuous use with only a five-year rest is practicable. In populated areas of highland Guatemala, almost all of the available land may be cleared or in second-growth. Several kinds of maize are planted over the year; tilling is by furrowing and, after the sprouts have appeared, by making hillocks. In these maize fields, or *milpas*, secondary crops like beans and squashes, or sweet manioc, are inter-planted, as well as chili peppers of many sizes, colours, and degrees of 'hotness'. In summary, while it utilizes the same kinds of plants as in the lowlands, the highland system of agriculture seems to be well adapted to an area of high population with good, deep soils where the competition posed by heavy forests and weeds is not a major problem.

But it is the lowlands (plate 1) lying to the north which are of most concern to the story of Maya civilization. A greater contrast with the highland environment could hardly be imagined, as every tourist flying to the ruins of Tikal from Guatemala City must have realized. The Petén-Yucatán peninsula is a single, great limestone shelf jutting up into the blue waters of the Gulf of Mexico which borders it on the west and north; its reef-girt eastern shores face the Caribbean. These limestones have risen from the sea over an immense period of time. In the older Petén region of the south, the up-lift has been greatest, and the topography is more rugged with broken karst hills rising above the plain. As one moves north to Yucatán itself, the country becomes flatter – it looks like a featureless, green carpet from the air – but this is deceptive for on foot the pitting of the porous limestone is all too apparent. In the northern reaches of our peninsula, about the only topo-graphical variation of any note is the Puuc range, a chain of low hills no more than a few hundred feet high strung out like an inverted 'V' across northern Campeche and south-western Yucatán.

Unlike the sierra to the south, there are few permanently flowing rivers in the lowlands, except in the west and in the south-east, where extensive alluvial bottom-lands have been formed. The great Usumacinta with its tributaries is the most important system, draining the northern highlands of Guatemala and the Lacandón country of Chiapas, twisting to the north-west past many a ruined Maya 'city' before depositing its yellow silts in the Gulf of Mexico. Sizeable rivers flowing into the Caribbean are the Motagua, which on its path to the sea cuts successively through pine and oak-clad hills, cactus-strewn desert, and tropical forest; the Belize River of British Honduras; and the Río Hondo which separates that former crown colony from Mexico.

Lakes are also rare in the lowlands, especially in the Yucatán Peninsula. The absence of ground water in many regions makes thirst a serious problem. In the Petén of northern Guatemala there are broad, swampy depressions or *bajos* which fill during the summer but are often dry in the rainless winter season. Smaller and similarly seasonal water-holes called *aguadas* are found in some places in Yucatán, but there the major source of drinking (and bathing) water for the inhabitants is the *cenote*, a word corrupted by the Spaniards from the Maya *dzonot*. These are circular sink holes, some of great size, formed by the collapse of underground caves. Because they are perennially filled with water percolating through the limestone, they necessarily have served as the focal points for native settlement since the first occupation of the land.

The lowland climate is hot, uncomfortably so towards the close of the dry season. In May come the rains, which last through October, but compared to other tropical regions of the world these are not especially abundant. In much of the Petén, for instance, only about seventy to ninety inches fall each year, and as one moves north to Yucatán there is a steady decrease from even this level. Nor is there total reliability in these rains, for in bad years there may be severe droughts. Really heavy precipitation is found in the far south of the Petén and British Honduras; in the Lacandón country of Chiapas; and in the Tabasco plains which are covered with great sheets of water during much of the summer and for that reason were largely shunned by the pre-Conquest Maya.

A high monsoon forest covers the southern lowlands, dominated by mahogany trees (plate 1) towering up to 150 feet above the jungle floor, by sapodillas, which gave wood to the ancients and chewing gum to ourselves and by the breadnut tree. In the middle and lower layers of this formation grow many fruit trees important to the Maya, such as the avocado. The forest is only partly evergreen, however, for in the dry season many species drop their leaves; but in a few places favoured by higher rainfall, there is real, non-deciduous rain forest.

Interspersed in the monsoon forest, particularly in the Petén and southern Campeche, are open savannahs covered with coarse grasses and dotted with stunted, flat-topped trees. There is no real agreement on the origin of the savannahs, but modern opinion is against the idea that they were created by the ancient Maya through over-cultivation of the land. On the other hand, they are certainly maintained by the hand of man, for while they are avoided by farmers they are periodically burned off by hunters so as to attract game to new grasses which sprout in the ashes.

To the north and west, where there is a profound drop in the annual rainfall, the forest turns into a low, thorny jungle, finally reaching the status of xerophytic scrub along the northern shore of the Yucatán Peninsula.

There is a rich fauna in the lowlands, although in the more heavily forested portions such as the Petén game is paradoxically scarcer than to the north. Deer and peccary abound, especially in Yucatán, which the Maya called 'The Land of the Turkey and the Deer'. Spider monkeys and the diminutive but noisy howler monkeys are easy to hunt and well favoured in the native cuisine. Among the larger birds are the ocellated turkey, with its beautiful golden-green plumage, the currasow, and the guan. More dangerous beasts are the jaguar, largest of the world's spotted cats, which was pursued for its resplendent pelt, and the water-loving tapir, killed both for its meat and for an incredibly tough hide employed in making shields and armour for Maya warriors.

Of more importance to the development of Maya civilization is the agricultural potential of the lowlands, which is by no means uniform. While the soils of the Petén, for instance, are relatively deep and fertile, those of Yucatán are the reverse. The sixteenth-century Franciscan bishop, Diego de Landa, our great authority on all aspects of Maya life, tells us that 'Yucatán is the country with least earth that I have seen, since all of it is one living rock and has wonderfully little earth'. It is little wonder that the early colonial chronicles speak much of famines in Yucatán before the arrival of the Spaniards, and it might be that the province relied less upon plant husbandry than upon its famed production of honey, salt, and slaves.

It is now almost universally recognized, if unwillingly, that tropical soils which are permanently deprived of their forest cover quickly decline in fertility and become quite unworkable as a layer of brick-like laterite develops on the surface. Tropical rainfall and a fierce sun do their destructive work in a surprisingly brief span, and agricultural disaster results. Under such conditions about the only kind of farming possible here in the Maya lowlands is that practised by the Maya themselves for many millennia – a shifting, slash-and-burn system under which the forest is permitted to regenerate at intervals. While seemingly simple, it requires great experience on the farmer's part. A patch of forest on well-drained land is chosen, and cut down in late autumn or early winter. The felled wood and brush are fired at the end of the dry season (plate 3), and all over the Maya lowlands the sun becomes obscured by the smoke and haze which cover the sky at that time. The maize seed is planted in holes poked through the ash with a dibble stick. Then the farmer must pray to the gods to bring the rain.

A *milpa* usually has a life of only two years, by which time decreasing yields no longer make it worthwhile to plant a third year. The Maya farmer must then shift to a new section of forest and begin again, leaving his old *milpa* fallow for periods which may be from four to seven years in the Petén, and from fifteen to twenty years in Yucatán. In inhabited regions the forest seen from the air looks like some great patchwork quilt of varying shades of green, a veritable mosaic of regenerating plots and new clearings.

In spite of what some pessimists have written, it now appears that this supposedly primitive method of wresting a living in a tropical forest milieu is a good deal more productive than it would seem at first glance, and it has been estimated that a single Petén farmer may support the food requirements of over twelve persons. Quite obviously, this figure bears upon the problem of the ancient population density of the Maya lowlands, and upon the question of what proportion of this population could have been released from their agricultural pursuits to engage as full-time participants in Maya civilization.

Areas

The Maya occupied three separate areas, which is hardly surprising considering the great environmental contrasts within the Maya realm (figure 1); Southern, Central, and Northern, the latter two entirely within the lowlands.

The Southern Area includes the highlands of Guatemala and adjacent Chiapas, together with the torrid coastal plain along the Pacific and the western half of El Salvador. In general, the Southern Area is somewhat aberrant (many books on the Maya ignore it altogether), almost surely because of the Mexican influence which has been very powerful here over a very long period of time. Some of the most characteristically 'Maya' traits are missing: the corbel vault in architecture and, except in Late Formative times, the Maya Long Count and the stela-altar complex. We must admit that in many ways the Southern Area hardly seems Maya at all from a purely archaeological standpoint, while some of it, such as the central and eastern Chiapas highlands, was only occupied by Maya-speakers at a relatively late date.

In the Central Area, on the other hand, Maya civilization soared to its greatest heights. Focused upon what is now the Department of Petén in northern Guatemala, it reaches from Tabasco and southern Campeche across the densely forested southern lowlands to include British Honduras, the Río Motagua of Guatemala, and a narrow portion of westernmost Honduras. All of the most typically 'Maya' traits are present – architectural features such as the corbel vault and roof comb, the fully developed Long Count with all its complexities, hieroglyphic writing, the stela-altar complex, and many others. These triumphs, however, were registered during the Classic period. Since the opening decades of the tenth century A.D., most of the area has been a green wilderness.

As one would expect, the Northern and Central Areas have much in common, since there are virtually no natural barriers to cultural exchange or to movements of peoples between the two. There is, none the less, a good deal of individuality to the Northern Area, due mainly to the circumstances that agricultural potentialities in Yucatán are poorer and that exactly where people may live is pretty much dictated by the distribution of cenotes, but also in part to Mexican influences which are almost as strong here as in the Southern Area. In contrast to the situation in the Petén, there was no abandonment of the Northern Area, and native population figures remain high.

Periods

The discovery of the ancient Maya civilization was a piecemeal process. Following the imposition of Spanish power in the Yucatán Peninsula, various persons such as the great Bishop Landa, or Fray Antonio de Ciudad Real who visited the famous site of Uxmal in 1588, wondered at the age of the mighty ruins which lay scattered across the land, but they could discover little from the natives. Real interest in Maya remains only began after the publication, in a London edition of 1822, of the brutal 'explorations' which Captain Del Río had inflicted upon the site of Palenque in the late eighteenth century. Modern Maya archaeology, however, stems from the epic journeys undertaken between 1839 and 1842 by the American diplomat and lawyer, John Lloyd Stephens, and his companion, the English topographical artist Frederick Catherwood, which revealed the full splendour of a vanished tropical civilization to the world.

Stephens and Catherwood were the first since Bishop Landa to assign the ruined 'cities' which they encountered to the actual inhabitants of the country – to the Maya Indians rather than to the peripatetic Israelites, Welshmen, Tartars, and so forth favoured by other 'authorities' – but they had no way of even roughly guessing at their age. It was not until the Maya calendrical script had been studied by Ernst Förstemann, the State Librarian of Saxony, and others, and the Maya inscriptions magnificently published by the Englishman Alfred P. Maudslay at the turn of the nineteenth century, that a real breakthrough was achieved in Maya chronology. In addition, large-scale excavations in Maya sites were begun at this time by the Peabody Museum of Harvard, to be followed by the Carnegie Institution of Washington, Tulane University, the University of Pennsylvania, and the Institute of Anthropology and History in Mexico.

The dating of the ancient Maya civilization now rests on four lines of evidence: 'dirt' archaeology itself, particularly the stratification of cultural materials like pottery; radiocarbon dating, in use since 1950; native historical traditions passed on to us by post-Conquest writers but bearing on the late pre-Conquest period; and the correct correlation of the Maya and Christian calendars.

The correlation problem is an unbelievably complex and still controversial topic which demands a few words of explanation. The Maya Long Count, which will be explained in greater detail in chapters 3 and 8, is an absolute, day-to-day calendar which has run like some great clock from some point in the distant past. Long Count dates were inscribed all over the ancient cities of the Central and Northern Areas. By the time of the Conquest, however, they were expressed in a very abbreviated and somewhat equivocal form. It is explicitly stated in the native chronicles (the so-called Books of Chilam Balam) that the Spanish foundation of Mérida, capital city of Yucatán, which in our calendar took place in January 1542, also fell shortly after the close of a specified period of the truncated Long Count. Bishop Landa, an impeccable source, tells us that a certain date in a more primitive Maya system, the fifty-two-year Calendar Round, fell on 26 July 1553 in our reckoning. All attempts to fit the Maya calendar to the Christian must take these two statements into account.

It so happens that there are only two correlations which meet these requirements as well as those of 'dirt' archaeology. These are the 11.16 or Thompson correlation, and the 12.9 or Spinden correlation, which would make all Maya dates 260 years earlier than does the former. Which of these is correct? The ancient Maya spanned the doorways of their temples with sapodilla wood beams (plate 40), and these have not only survived but can be dated by the radiocarbon process. A very long series of such samples has recently been run by the University of Pennsylvania, giving overwhelming support to the Thompson correlation. Most Mayanists have given sighs of relief, for any other chronology would play havoc with what we now think we know about the development of Maya culture over two millennia. Even further, any displacement in the dating of the Maya Classic period would disrupt the entire field of Mesoamerican research, for ultimately all archaeological chronologies in this part of the world are crosstied with the Maya Long Count.

As it now stands, the cultural sequence in the Maya area runs something like this. About the earliest occupation very little is known, but before 1500 B.C. there must have been simple horticulturalists and hunters following a way of life called 'Archaic', far better known for the upland peoples of Mexico. During the Formative Period, between 1500 B.C. and about A.D. 150, village farming became firmly established in all three areas, marking the first really intensive settlement of the Maya land. More advanced cultural traits like pyramid building and the inscribing of stone monuments are found by the terminal centuries of the Formative, while the short-lived Proto-Classic (A.D. 150–300) heralds the climax of Maya civilization in the lowlands. The spectacular Classic period, lasting from A.D. 300 to 900, is defined as that interval during which the lowland Maya were erecting stone monuments dated in the Long Count. A great cataclysm shook the lowlands around the close of the tenth century, at which time the Central Area was in large part abandoned, while the Northern and Southern Areas received the impact of Mexican invasions. Thus was inaugurated the Post-Classic, which endured until the arrival of the bearded adventurers from across the seas.

Peoples and Languages

While the cohesion of the Maya-speaking peoples is quite extraordinary for any time or place, the linguistic family called 'Mayan' contains a number of closely related but mutually unintelligible languages (figure 2), the result of a long period of internal divergence. A Maya from Yucatán would have the same trouble understanding an Indian from highland Chiapas as an Englishman would a Dutchman. There have been several attempts to correlate the various Mayan tongues in larger groups, but since in many cases we lack sufficiently large word lists as evidence, these can only be tentative. Professor McQuown proposes ten such groups; an ingenious method of vocabulary comparison called 'lexicostatistics' has enabled him and Maurice Swadesh to suggest approximate dates for the splitting-off of these from the ancestral Mayan language and from each other, a subject of considerable interest to archaeologists. Even if these dates proved to be wrong in absolute terms, they would be valid for the relative sequence of events.

McQuown believes that the very first Maya were a small

Indian tribe of North American origin, distantly affiliated with some peoples in southern Oregon and northern California, and more closely to the Totonacan and Zoquean speakers of Mexico. Moving south, they might have become settled in the highlands of western Guatemala by the middle of the third millennium B.C. During the next thousand years, the Huastec and the Yucatec split from the parent body, the former moving to the north-west and eventually to the Gulf Coast states of Tamaulipas and Veracruz, where they became completely separated from their linguistic kinsmen. The Yucatec migrated to the north, occupying the broad lowland plains of the Petén-Yucatán peninsula. The few hundred remaining Lacandón – primitive Maya who wear their hair long and still use the bow and arrow – inhabiting the Chiapas jungles south-west of the Usumacinta are pathetic survivors of a larger group which began diverging from Yucatec about this time, but which was probably always marginal to the major tribes.

Two more significant language groups broke away from the Maya homeland in the first half of the first millennium B.C., the Cholans and the Tzeltalans, moving down into the Central Area where they maintained close contact with each other and with the Yucatec to the north. The subsequent history of the Tzeltalans is fairly well known from linguistics and archaeology, for they seem to have left the Central Area by about A.D. 400 and returned to the highlands, pioneering the settlement of the mountain valleys around San Cristóbal de Las Casas, Chiapas. There many thousands of their descendants, the Tzotzil and Tzeltal, maintain unchanged old Maya patterns of life.

Other Mayan tongues have been more conservative and stay-at-home: the very archaic Mamean of western Guatemala which has spilled down to the Pacific coast in relatively late times, and the little-known Chuh, Kanhobalan, and Motozintlec

Huastecan
Cholan
Tzeltalan
Chuh
Kanhobalan
Motozintlec
Mamean
Quichean
Kekchian
Maya proper

YUCATEC

NAHUATL

CHONTAL

0   40   100   200 K.
0   50   100

Figure 2. Distribution of language groups

groups. But much of the late pre-Conquest history of the Southern Area concerns the powerful Quiché and Cakchiquel; they and their relatives, the Tzutuhil, who live in villages along the shores of the volcano-girt Lake Atitlán, speak languages which only a thousand years ago were one, Quichean. Since the Spanish Conquest, a more dominant role has been taken by the Kekchi, who have expanded from a centre in the Alta Verapaz of Guatemala to colonize southern British Honduras and the once Chol-speaking lowlands around Lake Izabal, Guatemala.

What, then, was the language recorded by the ancient Maya inscriptions and books? A glance at the linguistic map will show that the Yucatán Peninsula is occupied by Yucatec to the exclusion of all others, and there can be no quibbling that this was the speech of the Maya scribes of the Northern Area. It will also be seen that most of the Central Area is a blank, with the exception of those lands occupied by the Lacandón, by the surely recent Kekchi, and by certain Yucatec who are known to have moved into the Petén from the north no earlier than the thirteenth century A.D. and probably a good deal later. The idea that the language of the inscriptions of the Central Area was Yucatec has little to recommend it.

Some years ago Eric Thompson proposed that the Central Area was inhabited by Cholan-speakers during the Classic period. From its present distribution alone – with Chontal and Chol in the low hills and plains in the north-west, and Chorti in the south-east – it seems certain that Cholan once predominated across a great arc extending right through the Central Area, and we have some Spanish documents which confirm this point. The Mopan language of southern British Honduras, which some have wrongly placed with Yucatec in Maya proper, more certainly belongs with Cholan, strengthening the case, and it is hardly coincidental that Chol is still spoken around the Classic site of Palenque, and Chorti in the vicinity of Copán.

It seems inescapable, therefore, that the great civilization of the Central Area was the creation of Cholan Maya, although during the Early Classic some Tzeltalans may have played a part, and perhaps also ancestors of the mysterious Lacandón.

Languages other than Mayan are found in isolated pockets, indicating either intrusions of peoples from foreign lands or remnant populations engulfed by the expansion of the Mayan tongues. The somewhat shadowy Pipil, whose speech is very close to Náhuatl, the official language of the Aztec Empire, are concentrated in western El Salvador, but there are other Pipil communities on the Pacific coast and in the Motagua valley of Guatemala. Some authorities think that they invaded the Maya country from Mexico during the Toltec disruptions of the Early Post-Classic, an idea which is not out of line with the lexicostatistic evidence on them, but they could have come earlier. Tiny populations of Zoquean speakers near the Pacific coast in the Chiapas-Guatemala border region are probably vestiges of a once more widespread distribution of this language family. Xincan, with no known affiliations, seems to have extended over all of the eastern part of the Pacific coastal plain before the arrival of Mayan and Pipil, but the Xincan territory is an archaeological and ethnological blank. Náhuatl itself, as a great trading *lingua franca*, was spoken at the time of the Conquest at the port of Xicalango on the Laguna de los Términos in southern Campeche.

[2] The Earliest Maya

The Popol Vuh, a great epic of the Quiché Maya, recounts that the forefather gods, Tepeu and Gucumatz, brought forth the earth from a watery void, and endowed it with animals and plants. Anxious for praise and veneration after the creation, the divine progenitors fashioned man-like creatures from mud, but to mud they returned. Next a race of wooden figures appeared, but the mindless manikins were destroyed by the gods, to be replaced by men made from flesh. These, however, turned to wickedness and were annihilated as black rains fell and a great flood swept the earth. Finally true men, the ancestors of the Quiché, were created from maize dough.

Neither tradition nor archaeology have thrown much light on Maya origins. Tribal memories are weak, and a combination of luxuriant vegetation and unfavourable geological conditions has made the search for really early remains difficult. There are few caves and rock-shelters suitable for habitation by primitive hunters and gatherers (figure 3), and open sites are almost impossible to detect, especially in the monsoon forests.

Early Hunters

We can only guess when the first settlement of the Maya area took place. The initial colonization of the New World was made by Asiatic peoples crossing over the Bering Straits land bridge towards the end of the Pleistocene, or Ice Age. By the ninth millennium B.C., the first Indians were already camped on the wind-swept Straits of Magellan, at the southern tip of South America, and so we may assume that primitive hunters had by then occupied all that part of the Americas that was worth inhabiting. Large areas of both continents were grassland over which roamed great herds of herbivores – mammoths, horses, camels, and giant bison.

In the United States, Canada, and Alaska, where a number of camps belonging to this ancient epoch have been located, the earliest culture which has stood up to archaeological scrutiny is called Clovis, well dated to about twelve to ten thousand years ago. If we can rely upon the remains in several slaughtering sites in the American south-west, the Clovis people lived mainly off mammoth-hunting, although in lean times they must have been content with more humble foods. These great elephants were killed with darts hurled from spear-throwers, fitted with finely chipped and 'fluted' points from the bases of which long channel flakes had been removed on one or both faces. Clovis points are widely distributed, from Alaska to Nova Scotia, down through Mexico and into Central America. They have even been found in Costa Rica and Panama.

Thus far the earliest known artifact from Maya country is a small projectile point of obsidian (plate 5), found by a picnicking schoolboy at San Rafael, in the pine-clad hills just west of Guatemala City. Even a neophyte would recognize this as a Clovis: fluting has been carried out on one side, the edges are ground down where the object was to be lashed to a dart or spear shaft. It is remarkably similar in outline to several such points which have been collected in Mexico, and to the smaller Clovis points of the United States. From this isolated find we can only conclude that early hunters were roaming the Maya

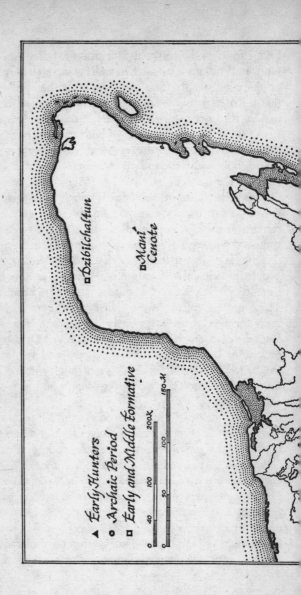

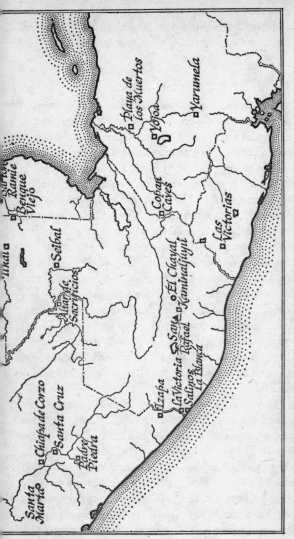

Figure 3. Sites of Early Hunters, Archaic, and Early and Middle Formative Periods

highlands during the late Ice Age, and that the future will probably see much more evidence for this early era.

Archaic Collectors and Cultivators

By about 7000 B.C. the ice sheets which had covered much of North America in the higher latitudes were in full retreat, and during the next five and a half thousand years the climate of the world was everywhere warmer than it is today. In Europe this interval has been called the 'Climatic Optimum', but in many parts of the New World conditions were by no means so favourable, least of all for hunters. A fatal combination of hot, dry weather, which turned grasslands into desert, and over-hunting by man had finished off the big game. In upland Mexico the Indians were diverted to another way of life, based on an intensified collection of the seeds and roots of wild plants, and upon the killing of smaller, more solitary animals. In their economy, in their semi-nomadic pattern of settlement, and even in the details of their tool-kits the Mexican Indians of the Archaic period were only part of the 'Desert Culture', extending at that time all the way from southern Oregon, through the Great Basin of the United States (where it survived into the nineteenth century), and down into southeastern Mexico.

It was in Mexico, however, and in this 'Desert Culture' context, that all of the important plant foods of Mesoamerica – maize, beans, squashes, chili peppers, and many others – were first domesticated. Excavations in dry caves of the Tehuacán Valley, in the Puebla Highlands of Mexico, have shown that the grass ancestral to modern maize had been brought under man's control by 5000 B.C. It seems likely that the practice of plant cultivation must have reached the Maya area at some time during the Archaic period. Not so very long ago it was firmly believed that the Maya themselves had been the first to domesticate Indian corn (*Zea mays*) but this idea was rooted on the false premise that the wild progenitor of maize was *teosinte*, a common weed in Guatemalan cornfields which has since proved to be the bastard offspring of domestic maize and tripsacum, a distant relative of maize. None the less Guatemala (which is no larger than the state of Ohio) has more distinct varieties of maize than can be found in all of the United States put together, arguing that this must have been a very old centre for the evolution of this plant under the tutelage of man. Quite probably all of the uplands, from southern Mexico through Chiapas and highland Guatemala, were involved in the processes leading to the modern races of this most productive of all food plants.

It will be recalled that, according to lexicostatistic dating, the ancestral Maya had arrived in the Chiapas-Guatemala highlands by about 2500 B.C., well within the Archaic span and before the most ancient known pottery-using cultures, and it may have been they who brought maize and other cultigens to our area. Beyond the western border of the Maya area the rock shelter of Santa Marta (figure 3) in Chiapas may record traces of this *ur*-Maya group. Unfortunately, somewhat wetter conditions than those in the Tehuacán Valley have destroyed any perishables which might have been left by the ancient inhabitants of the shelter, but nut-cracking stones with pecked depressions, and pebble *manos* (handstones) and metates (querns) tell us that seeds and other plant foods were well exploited. Other artifacts of the Santa Marta Complex, including chipped projectile points, choppers, and scrapers, strongly resemble those of the Tehuacán and Tamaulipas caves, and the whole assemblage, which is estimated to last from 7000 to 3500 B.C., obviously belongs with the Mexican Archaic and more generally with the 'Desert Culture'.

A Late Archaic site more properly within the Maya highlands is El Chayal, an obsidian (figure 4) workshop scattered over the tops and slopes of several hills to the south-east of Guatemala City, in a region where natural deposits of obsidian are plentiful. The surface is strewn with many thousands of large, coarse blades struck from crude cores, probably as

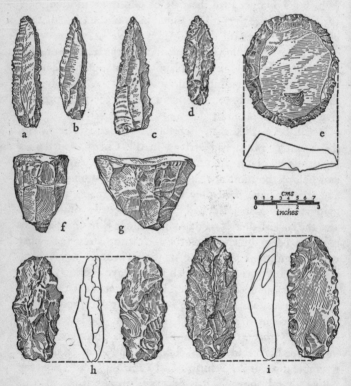

Figure 4. Obsidian artifacts from El Chayal, Guatemala. a–b, large flake-blades; c, unifacial knife; d, stemmed projectile point; e, scraping plane; f–g, cores; h–i, bifacial tools

'blanks' in a semi-finished state to be worked elsewhere into points for darts and spears or into knives. No digging has been carried out at this odd site, but some of the completed artifacts picked up there recall terminal Archaic cultures in Mexico, particularly some simple, stemmed projectile points, crude choppers, and enormous disk-shaped scrapers the use of which remains a mystery. If the evidence for the Archaic period is poor in the highlands, it is even worse in the Maya lowlands. Yet we have some idea of what the Petén looked like then, based on analysis of wind-blown pollen recovered from a long core drilled into the bottom of Lake Petenxil, in the heart of the Central Area. It used to be thought that the savannahs which punctuate the tropical forest had resulted from an over-use of their fields by the Classic Maya, with a consequent invasion of unwanted grasses. This notion has now been turned upside-down. At 2000 B.C., the Petén was like a parkland, with broad savannahs surrounded by copses of oak, the tropical forest being considerably more restricted than at present. The strong dominance of forest over grasslands has been shown to have begun only during the Classic Period (A.D. 300–900), reaching peak intensity after the Maya had fairly deserted the Petén.

The same pollen core has also provided an unexpected bit of information, namely that by 2000 B.C. a little maize was being grown near the margins of the lake, a good thousand years before the first pottery-using farmers are known for the region. Who were these people? If we accept the word of the linguists, they could have been the Yucatec, on their trek north to Yucatán from the Maya homeland, but since their sites have not been located this is mere speculation. While some African peoples raise their crops in tropical grasslands, it is unlikely that the pioneer Maya, lacking metal tools, could have tilled the savannahs. More plausibly, they would have colonized patches of tropical forest which offered good soils and the possibility of clearing by the slash-and-burn method, avoiding the open country as assiduously as did the early Neolithic farmers of Europe.

The Archaic, then, remains a dim, shadowy epoch, but one during which the genesis of Maya culture must have taken place.

Early Formative Villages

Really effective farming, in the sense that densely inhabited villages were now to be found throughout the Maya area, was an innovation of the Formative Period, which lasted from 1500 B.C. to about A.D. 150. What brought it about? Some scholars favour the theory that it was a major improvement in the productivity of the maize plant, perhaps through back-crossing with its vigorous offspring, *teosinte*. At any rate, villages made up of thatched-roof houses, in no wise different from those in use among the modern Maya peasantry, now dotted the land.

Still, we must not assume that the advance to Formative life took place everywhere at the same time. Rather, it is in those environments which abounded on the one hand in easily obtained wild animal and plant foods, and on the other in fertile and workable soils, that a precocious development of permanently occupied villages is to be expected.

One such ecological zone is the Pacific littoral of Guatemala, near the Chiapas frontier. This region may not have been Maya-speaking in ancient times, but its early cultures must bear a likeness to the sort of evolution towards fully settled life that some day will be found elsewhere in the Maya area. In that hot, fertile land the oldest village culture is Ocós (figure 5), which may begin by 1500 B.C., followed by Cuadros (fixed by radiocarbon dates to 1000–850 B.C.), both of which are

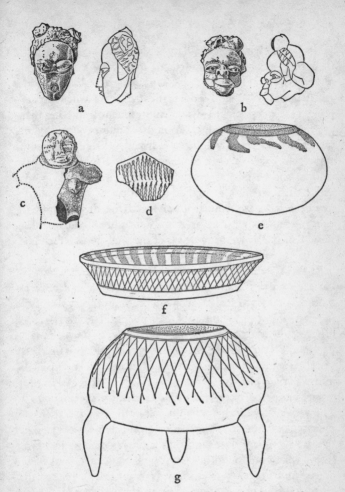

Figure 5. Figurines and reconstructed vessels of the Ocós culture (Early
Formative Period). a–c, fragments of pottery figurines; d, fragment of neckless
pottery jar, with rocker-stamping; e, neckless jar with red paint on rim and
body; f, bowl with striping in iridescent paint on interior; g, tripod neckless
jar with iridescent paint on rim. a, 2½ in. high; b, c, to scale; d, 2½ in. wide;
e, 9 in. wide; f, g, to scale

Early Formative. In those days settlements were little more than tiny hamlets of some three to twenty families each, placed just above the muddy banks of mangrove-lined estuaries and lagoons. The Early Formative villagers efficiently exploited the rich, brackish-water environment, gathering mangrove oysters and marsh clams in great numbers, and taking turtles and crabs, while iguanas (a harmless lizard of fearsome appearance) were caught for their tasty flesh and eggs. In the lagoons and near-by rivers they fished for gar, snook, porgy, and catfish. In slightly higher lands adjacent to their settlements they cleared the tropical forest for their cornfields; cobs miraculously preserved in the débris of a Cuadros village show that the maize grown was of the well-known race Nal-Tel, still favoured by many lowland Maya farmers.

The scarcity or in some cases complete absence in Ocós and Cuadros sites of bones from animals which would have required an effort to secure, such as deer and peccary, testify to the sit-at-home propensities of these people. The arts of settled life were allowed to flourish, particularly pottery which makes its first appearance in the Maya area at this time. But fired clay vessels are known even earlier than this in Mexico, especially in the Purrón phase at Tehuacán, where an extremely crude, gravel-tempered ware was manufactured by about 2000 B.C. The interesting thing about Purrón pottery is that there are only two shapes: the *tecomate*, or globular, neckless jar, and the flat-bottomed dish with outslanting sides. It is just those forms which are found in the ground-stone containers of the preceding culture, Abejas, and it is reasonable to assume that regardless of where the *idea* of firing clay originated, the first Mesoamerican ceramics were evolved in part from prototypes in stone.

It is no surprise then to find *tecomates* and flat-bottomed bowls the predominant shapes of Ocós (figure 5) and Cuadros, as they are of other Early Formative cultures elsewhere in Mesoamerica, such as the related Chiapa I or Cotorra phase of central Chiapas. Quite unexpected, however, is the surprising sophistication of Ocós ceramics: the most unusual plastic techniques are used to embellish surfaces, the roughened zones usually contrasting with the smooth, and on many vessels a deep red, sparkling slip made from specular hematite was applied. Rocker-stamping (figure 5d) was often carried out with the crinkly edge of a shell, by 'walking' the edge of the shell in zigzags across the wet clay. But two kinds of decoration deserve special mention. Many Ocós potsherds were found to have been impressed with cord or twine (sometimes so fine, it must have been a cotton thread) which had been wrapped around a paddle. Cord-marking is known on Neolithic ceramics in much of the Old World, and is characteristic of the first pottery in northern North America; its appearance in Ocós, thus far unique for Mesoamerica, cannot yet be explained. Another oddity is the use of a special glossy clay slip (figure 5 f, g), giving a coppery-metallic sheen when seen at the right angle, known elsewhere only on the coast of Ecuador during the Formative Period.

Less spectacular artifacts – stone *manos* and *metates* for grinding maize kernels into dough, notched potsherds utilized as weights for fishnets, and so forth – belong to the mundane life of the period. There is another element already present in Ocós culture which is worthy of mention, ceremonialism. In Ocós débris at La Victoria, we found a number of solid, hand-made female figurines of pottery. Such objects were made by the thousands in many later Formative villages of both Mexico and the Maya area, and while nobody is exactly sure of their meaning, it is generally thought that they had something to do with the fertility of crops, in much the same way as did the Mother Goddess figurines of Neolithic and Bronze age Europe. For the New World, the earliest appear by 3000 B.C. in Ecuador and it may be that those of Mesoamerica were ultimately derived from that direction.

Every Ocós house, its pole walls daubed with mud and whitewashed, was raised above the ground on a low, earthen platform so as to avoid the inundations of the summer rainy period. In an Ocós site not very far from La Victoria is a much larger mound, reaching a height of about twenty-five feet, so lofty that it surely was a temple platform. All temples in pre-Spanish Mesoamerica, even the towering pyramids of the Maya Lowlands, are essentially nothing more than a magnification of the humble peasant dwelling – the simple, rectangular house on its own flat mound. Far back in time, near the very beginnings of Formative life, the adoption of completely sedentary ways had given rise not only to full- or part-time specialists in the arts of pottery, weaving, and the like, but also to religious practitioners. Perhaps at first only the houses of leading persons in the community were used for their rites; eventually, a more grandiose structure was built for the purpose, raised up higher and higher to the sky by enlarging the supporting mound, finally resulting in a temple to which several of the surrounding villages could have been drawn. As ordinary men were buried beneath the floors of their own houses, so the great men of the élite class began to be interred inside the platforms of these temples. The evidence at hand suggests that this could have taken place already by Ocós times.

Away from the Pacific coast very little was known until recently about the Early Formative. It is possible that a deep layer of broken water jars, bearing a surprising resemblance to Roman amphorae, which was uncovered by the late George Brainerd on the edge of a *cenote* at Maní, in Yucatán, belongs to this horizon, since it underlies pottery typical of the Middle

Formative Period. In the highlands the *tecomate*-using Arévalo people, known from a modest excavation at Kaminaljuyú on the outskirts of Guatemala City, can be best placed as late in the Early Formative (*c.* 850 B.C.).

In contrast to the simple picture which we have been painting for the Early Formative, we now know that a great culture was already coexistent with these humble, farming villagers. This was the brilliant Olmec civilization of the hot, coastal plain of southern Veracruz and adjacent Tabasco, which according to the latest archaeological information had begun to take shape by 1200 B.C. at the important centre of San Lorenzo. The abruptness of its appearance on the scene has no convincing explanation at the present moment. Suffice it to say that built on a cultural base not unlike Ocós and Cuadros was a remarkable artistic, social, and presumably political complex. The main Olmec influence upon the Maya peoples, however, did not take effect until the succeeding Middle Formative Period.

The Middle Formative Expansion

If conditions before 800 B.C. were perhaps not optimum for the spread of effective village farming except for a few favoured regions, in the following centuries the reverse must have been true. Heavy populations, all with pottery, began to establish themselves in both highlands and lowlands during the Middle Formative Period, which lasted until about 300 B.C. In no instance do we have remains suggesting that these were anything more than simple peasants: there was no writing, little that could be called architecture, and hardly any development of art. In fact, nothing but a rapidly mounting population would make us think that the Maya in this period were very different from their immediate ancestors.

This is in strong contrast to the Olmec civilization which was then flourishing along the Gulf Coast, to the west of the Maya area, and which reached its peak towards the end of the Middle Formative and then collapsed as suddenly as did the Maya at a much later time. After the decline of San Lorenzo, about 900 B.C., the great Olmec centre was La Venta, situated on an island in the midst of the swampy wastes of the lower Tonalá River. La Venta was dominated by a 100-foot-high temple pyramid of clay. Elaborate tombs and spectacular offerings of jade and serpentine figurines were concealed by various constructions, both there and at other Olmec sites. The Olmec art style, as seen in gigantic basalt sculptures (some weighing many tons) and in smaller carvings, was centred upon the representation of a creature which combined the features of a snarling jaguar with those of a weeping human infant; this were-jaguar almost surely was a rain god, the first recognizable deity of the Mesoamerican pantheon. From the unity of the art style, from the size and beauty of the sculptured monuments, and from the massive scale of the public architecture there can be no doubt that there was a powerful Olmec state on the Gulf Coast which even at this early time was able to command enormous resources both in manpower and in materials.

More important to the study of the Maya, there are also good reasons to believe that it was the Olmec who devised the elaborate Long Count calendar, and the Olmec who invented writing. Whether or not one thinks of the Olmec as the 'mother culture' of Mesoamerica, the fact is that many other civilizations, including the Maya, were ultimately dependent on the Olmec achievement. This is especially true during the Middle Formative, when lesser peasant cultures away from the Gulf Coast were acquiring traits which had filtered to them from their more advanced neighbours, just as in ancient

Europe barbarian peoples in the west and north eventually had the benefits of the achievements of the contemporaneous Bronze Age civilizations of the Near East.

One of the greatest of all archaeological sites in the New World is Kaminaljuyú (figure 12), on the western margins of Guatemala City in a broad, fertile valley lying athwart the Continental Divide. Although it consisted of several hundred great temple mounds in Maudslay's day, all but a handful have been swallowed up by the rapidly expanding slums and real-estate developments of the capital. Rescue operations by the Carnegie Institution of Washington have shown that whereas part of the site was constructed during the Early Classic, the great majority of the mounds were definitely Formative. The loss to science through the depredations of brickyards and bulldozers has been incalculable.

It has been no easy task, under these circumstances, to work out an archaeological succession for Kaminaljuyú, but the oldest culture is probably Arévalo, for which we have little more than some sherds from *tecomates* and red-slipped bowls. This is followed by Las Charcas, which marks a major occupation of the Valley of Guatemala, for Las Charcas remains are scattered widely. Its stratigraphic position underneath deposits of the Late Formative, backed up by a number of slightly contradictory radiocarbon dates, suggests that this village culture falls towards the end of the Middle Formative, around the fifth or fourth century B.C.

The best-preserved Las Charcas remains come from a series of bottle-shaped pits which had been cut in ancient times down through the topsoil into the underlying volcanic ash. No one has a firm idea of the purpose of these excavations. Perhaps some may have been cooking pits, and it is entirely possible that as among the historic Hidatsa Indians of the Great Plains others may have been for the storage of maize and beans, but surely their final use was as refuse containers. In them have been found carbonized avocado seeds, maize cobs, and remnants of textiles, basketry and probably mats, and rope fragments. The magnificent Las Charcas white ware (figure 6), manufactured from a kaolin-like clay, is extremely

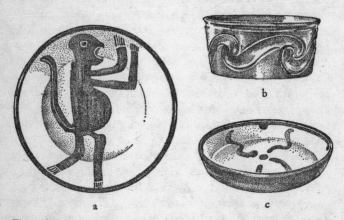

Figure 6. Pottery vessels of the Las Charcas culture, Middle Formative Period. a, c, interiors of red-on-white bowls; b, grey-brown bowl with modelled decoration. a, 12 in. diam.; b, c, to scale

sophisticated, with designs in red showing spider monkeys with upraised arms, grotesque dragon masks, and other more abstract motifs. Las Charcas figurines (plate 4) are predominantly female, but with a liveliness of concept seldom found elsewhere. Again, as with coeval cultures in other parts of Mesoamerica, there is good evidence for the construction of clay temple mounds of considerable size, perhaps already arranged around plazas.

In the Maya Lowlands, both in the Central and in the Northern Areas, we now have for the first time substantial evidence for a Maya population. The oldest occupation, the little-known Xe culture, appears in deep levels at the site of Altar de Sacrificios and at Seibal in the western part of the Petén, and may represent some kind of intrusion from the Highlands via the Lacantún drainage system. But it is in the northern Petén where the Middle Formative has been best defined. Considerable excavations at the great Maya centres of Uaxactún and Tikal have shown that Mamom is the dominant culture of this time, and have thus far failed to turn up anything substantially earlier. It should be kept in mind that the Petén may have been no promised land for more ancient peoples intruding into it, particularly if annual rainfall was at one time somewhat below its present amount.

Mamom, which has a radiocarbon date within the fifth century B.C., looks like a simple village culture since no examples of public architecture have yet been revealed by the archaeologist's spade, but the special conditions of excavations in the Petén must be considered. The lowland Maya almost always built their temples over older ones, so that in the course of centuries the earliest constructions would eventually come to be deeply buried within the towering accretions of rubble and plaster. Consequently, to prospect for Mamom temples in one of the larger sites would be extremely costly in time and labour, and the question of their existence should be kept open.

Mamom pottery is quite simple when compared to Las Charcas, with which it is related. The commonest wares are red and orange-red monochromes, with polychrome decoration absent. Usually the only embellishment is simple incising on the inside of bowls, or daubing of necked jars with red blobs. The figurine cult, if such it may be called, is present in Mamom, with a wide range of stylistic treatment carried out by punching and with applied strips of clay. At Tikal, a cache of Mamom ceramics was discovered in a sealed *chultun*. This is a bottle-shaped chamber below the plaza floor, quite comparable in shape and perhaps in use to those of Las Charcas. Chultuns are ubiquitous in sites of the Central and Northern Areas, cut down into the limestone marl from the surface. We know that by the Late Classic, they were used for burials and reach some degree of elaboration; they also seem to have functioned as sweat baths. Initially, however, they could have been utilized as sources of the fine *sascab* lime employed in construction by Maya architects, but their use as storage pits should not be overlooked. Whatever the answer to the 'chultun mystery', they are as old as the Mamom phase.

Something like Mamom has been found throughout the Maya Lowlands wherever serious excavations have been undertaken – even at the site of Dzibilchaltun (figure 3) in northern Yucatán.

The Middle Formative sees the establishment of Maya-speaking peasants everywhere; the flowering of Maya culture could only have taken place on this base. But there is absolutely nothing to suggest that Maya civilization as we understand it – the vaulted masonry architecture, the naturalistic painting and relief style, Long Count calendar and hieroglyphic writing – had even begun to germinate during this epoch.

[3] The Rise of Maya Civilization

It is a long step from the village cultures that we have thus far been considering to the awe-inspiring achievements of the Classic Maya, but by no means an impossible one. The all-important questions are, what happened during the intervening time covered by the Late Formative and Proto-Classic Periods, and how did those traits considered as typical of the Classic Maya actually develop?

There have been a number of contradictory theories to account for the rise of Maya civilization (figure 7). One of the most persistent holds that the previously undistinguished Maya came under the influence of travellers from shores as distant as the China coast; as a matter of interest to the lay public, it should be categorically emphasized that *no* objects manufactured in any part of the Old World have been identified in any Maya site, and that ever since the days of Stephens and Catherwood theories involving trans-Pacific or trans-Atlantic contact have never survived scientific scrutiny. Another school of thought holds that because of the supposedly low agricultural potential of the Petén and Yucatán, civilization was introduced to the lowlands from an outside area with a more favourable ecology. There are others who claim that this potential has been gravely underrated, and that Maya culture as it is known for the Classic Period is completely *sui generis*, with no trace of outside influence. Needless to say, both of these points of view are overstated, and both are at least

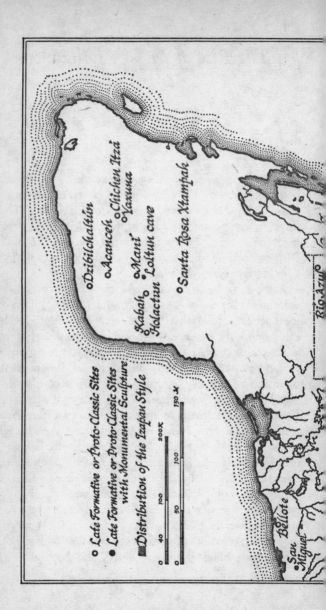

Late Formative or Proto-Classic Sites

Late Formative or Proto-Classic Sites
with Monumental Sculpture

Distribution of the Izapan Style

oDzibilchaltun

oAcanceh
oChichen Itza
oYaxuna

oMani
Kabah Loltun cave
oHolactun

oSanta Rosa Xtampak

Rio Azul

Bellote

San
Miguel

Figure 7. Sites of the Late Formative and Proto-Classic Periods

partly wrong. The fact is that the Maya of both highlands and lowlands have never been isolated from the rest of Meso-america, and that Mexican influences have sporadically guided the course of Maya cultural history since very early times, as we shall see in this and subsequent chapters.

How are we to define the word 'civilization'? How do the civilized differ from the barbaric? Archaeologists have usually dodged this question by offering lists of traits which they think to be important. Cities are one criterion, but as we shall find, neither the Classic Maya nor a number of other early civilizations had anything we can call by that name. The late V. G. Childe thought that writing should be another, but the obviously advanced Inca of Peru were completely illiterate. Civilization, in fact, is different in degree rather than in kind from what precedes it, but has certainly been achieved by the time that state institutions, large-scale public works, temple buildings, and widespread, unified art styles have appeared. With few exceptions, the complex state apparatus demands some form of records, and writing has usually been the answer; so has the invention of more-or-less accurate means of keeping time.

Yet all civilizations are in themselves unique. The Classic Maya of the lowlands had a very elaborate calendar; writing; temple pyramids and palaces of limestone masonry with vaulted rooms; architectural layouts emphasizing buildings arranged around plazas, with rows of stone stelae lined up before some; polychrome pottery; and a very sophisticated art style expressed in bas reliefs and in wall paintings. These traits are now known to have been developed in the Late Formative (300 B.C.–A.D. 150) and Proto-Classic (A.D. 150–300) Periods.

The Birth of the Calendar

Some system of recording time is essential to all higher cultures – to fix critical events in the lives of the persons ruling the state, to guide the agricultural and ceremonial year, and to record celestial motions. The Calendar Round of fifty-two years was present among all the Mesoamericans, including the Maya, and is presumably of very great age. It consists of two permutating cycles (figure 8). One is of 260 days, representing the intermeshing of a sequence of the numbers one through thirteen with twenty named days. Among the Maya, the 260-

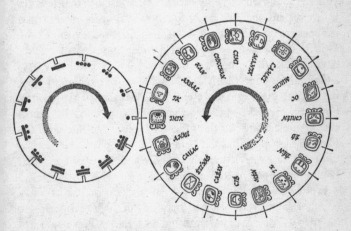

Figure 8. Schematic representation of the 260-day count

day count (sometimes called by the *ersatz* term '*tzolkin*') began with 1 Imix, followed by 2 Ik, 3 Akbal, 4 Kan, until 13 Ben had been reached; the day following was of course Ix, with the coefficient one again, leading to 2 Men, and so on. The last day of the cycle would be 13 Ahau, and it would repeat once again commencing with 1 Imix. How such a period of time ever came into being remains an enigma, but the use to which it was put is clear. Every single day had its own omens and associations, and the inexorable march of the twenty days acted as a kind of perpetual fortune-telling machine guiding the destinies of the Maya and of all the peoples of Mexico. It still survives in unchanged form among some isolated folk in southern Mexico and the Maya highlands, under the care of calendar priests.

Meshing with the 260-day count is a 'Vague Year' (figure 9) of 365 days, so called because the *actual* length of the solar year is about a quarter-day more, a circumstance that leads us to intercalate one day every four years to keep our calendar in march with the sun, but which was ignored by the Maya. Within it, there were eighteen named 'months' of twenty days each, with a much-dreaded interval of five unlucky days added at the end. The Maya New Year started with 1 Pop, the next day being 2 Pop, etc. The final day of the month, however, carried not the coefficient twenty, but a sign indicating the 'seating' of the month to follow, in line with the Maya philosophy that the influence of any particular span of time is felt *before* it actually begins and persists somewhat beyond its apparent termination.

From this it follows that a particular day in the 260-day count, such as 1 Kan, also had a position in the Vague Year, for instance 1 Pop. A day designated as 1 Kan 1 Pop could not return until 52 Vague Years (18,980 days) had passed. This is the Calendar Round (figure 10), and it is the only annual time count possessed by the highland peoples of Mexico, one that obviously has its disadvantages where events taking place over a span of more than fifty-two years are concerned.

Although it is usually assumed to be 'Maya', the Long Count was widely distributed in Classic and earlier times in the lowland country of Mesoamerica, but it was carried to its highest degree of refinement by the Maya of the Central Area. This is really another kind of permutation count, but the cycles used are so large that, unlike the Calendar Round, any event within the span of historical time could be fixed without fear of ambiguity. Instead of taking the Vague Year as the basis for the Long Count, the Maya and other peoples employed the *tun*, a period of 360 days. The Long Count cycles (figure 44) are

20 kins	1 uinal or 20 days
18 uinals	1 tun or 360 days
20 tuns	1 katun or 7,200 days
20 katuns	1 baktun or 144,000 days.

Long Count dates inscribed by the Maya on their monuments consist of the above cycles listed from top to bottom in descending order of magnitude, each with its numerical coefficient, and all to be added up so as to express the number of days elapsed since the end of the last Great Cycle, a period of 13 baktuns whose ending fell on the date 4 Ahau 8 Cumku. Thus, a Long Count date conventionally written as 9.10.19.5.11 10 Chuen 4 Cumku would be calculated as follows:

9 baktuns	1,296,000 days
10 katuns	72,000 days
19 tuns	6,840 days
5 uinals	100 days
11 kins	11 days

or 1,374,951 days since the close of the last Great Cycle, reaching the Calendar Round position 10 Chuen 4 Cumku.

 TZÉC

 YAX

 ZOTZ

 CHEN

 ZIP

 MOL

 UO

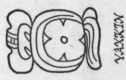 YAXKIN

 POP

 XUL

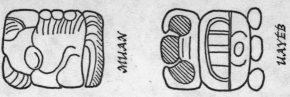

MUAN KANKIN MAC CEH ZAC

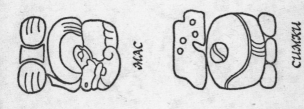

UAYEB CUMKU KAYAB PAX

Figure 9. Signs for the months in the 365-day count

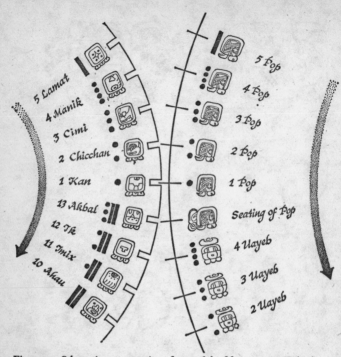

Figure 10. Schematic representation of part of the fifty-two-year Calendar Round

Something should also be said about the coefficients themselves (cf. figure 43). The Maya, along with a few other groups of the lowlands and the Mixtec of Oaxaca, had a number system of great simplicity, employing only three symbols: a dot with the value of 'one', a horizontal bar for 'five', and a stylized shell for 'nought'. Numerals up to four were expressed by dots only, six was a bar with a dot above, and ten two bars. Nineteen, the highest coefficient in calendrical use, took the form of four dots above three bars. The treatment of higher numbers, for which the 'nought' symbol was essential, will be discussed in chapter 8.

It is generally agreed that the Long Count must have been set in motion long after the inception of the Calendar Round, but by just how many centuries or millennia is uncertain. Be that as it may, the oldest recorded Long Count dates fall within Baktun 7, and appear on monuments (figure 7) which lie *outside* the Maya area. At present the most ancient seems to be Stela 2 at Chiapa de Corzo, a major ceremonial centre which had been in existence since Early Formative times in the dry Grijalva Valley of central Chiapas: in a vertical column are carved the numerical coefficients (7.16.)3.2.13, followed by the day 6 Ben, the 'month' of the Vague Year being suppressed as in all these early inscriptions. This would correspond to 9 December, 36 B.C. Five years later the famous Stela C at the Olmec site of Tres Zapotes in Veracruz was inscribed with (7.)16.6.16.18 6 Etz'nab. On both of these fragmentary monuments, the initial coefficients are missing but reconstructable.

Now, the 16th katun of Baktun 7 would fall within the Late Formative, and we can be sure that unless these dates are to be counted forward from some base *other* than 13.0.0.0.0 4 Ahau 8 Cumku (as the end of the last Great Cycle is sometimes recorded), which seems improbable, then the 'Maya' calendar had reached what was pretty much its final form by the first century B.C. among peoples who were under powerful Olmec influence and who may not even have been Maya. From them writing and the calendar were spread along the Pacific coast of Guatemala and into the Maya highlands, eventually reaching the developing states of the Petén forests.

Izapa and the Pacific Coast

Crucial to the problem of how higher culture came about among the Maya is the Izapan civilization (figure 7), for it occupies a middle ground in time and in space between the Middle Formative Olmec and the Early Classic Maya. Its hallmark is an elaborate art style, found on monuments scattered over a wide zone from Tres Zapotes on the Veracruz coast, to the Pacific plain of Chiapas and Guatemala, and up into the Guatemala City area.

Izapa itself is a very large site made up of over eighty temple mounds of earthen construction faced with river cobbles, just east of Tapachula, Chiapas, in the moist, slightly hilly country about twenty miles inland from the Pacific shore. Whether it belongs with Mexico, culturally speaking, or with the Maya area is debatable, but the tongue anciently spoken here was not Maya but Tapachulteco (figure 2), a vestigial member of the once more widespread Zoquean group. While Izapa was founded as a ceremonial centre as far back as Early Formative times and continued in use until the Early Classic, the bulk of the constructions and probably all of the many carved monuments belong to the Late Formative and Proto-Classic eras. The Izapan art style centres upon large, ambitiously conceived but somewhat cluttered scenes carried out in bas relief. Many of the activities shown are profane, such as a richly attired person decapitating a vanquished foe, but there are also deities, chief among whom is what may be called the 'Long-lipped God' (cf. plate 11). This being has an immensely extended upper lip and flaring nostril, and is surely a development of the old Olmec were-jaguar, the god of rain and lightning. Certain recurrent elements must represent well-understood iconographic motifs, such as a U-shaped form between diagonal bars above the principal scene, perhaps an early occurrence of the sky-band so ubiquitous in Classic Maya art; the 'U' itself is probably the prototype of the Maya glyph for the moon (figure 45d), and is found repeated many times on the same relief.

Izapa, then, is a major centre with some of the features which we consider more typical of the lowland Maya already in full flower – the stela-altar complex, the Long-lipped God who becomes transformed into the Maya rain god Chac, and a highly painterly, two-dimensional art style which emphasizes historical and mythic scenography with great attention to plumage and other costume details. Writing and the calendar are absent, but as one moves along the Pacific slopes east into Guatemala, one finds sites with inscribed monuments and Baktun 7 dates.

One of these Guatemalan stations is Abaj Takalik, south of Colomba in a lush, well-watered piedmont zone that in the days of the Conquest was a great producer of chocolate, and now is devoted to coffee. Like Izapa, it is made up of earthen mounds scattered about the site with little attention to formal arrangement. That the Olmec had once intruded here is apparent from a large boulder located less than a mile from the main group of mounds, carved in relief with a bearded werejaguar in the purest Olmec style. Stela 1 from the site is purely Izapan but dateless. On the other hand, Stela 2, now somewhat damaged, bore on its carved face two richly attired Izapan figures with tall, plumed head-dresses, facing each other across a vertical row of glyphs, below a cloud-like mass of volutes from which peers the face of a sky god. The topmost sign in the column is beyond doubt a very early form of the Introductory Glyph which in later Classic inscriptions stands at the head of a Long Count date. Just beneath is the baktun coefficient, which is pretty clearly the number seven.

A more complete Baktun 7 inscription appears on Stela 1 (figure 11), the 'Herrera Stela', from El Baúl, a coffee plantation considerably to the south-east of Abaj Takalik in a region studded with Early Classic centres of the Cotzumalhuapa culture. This object has attracted fairly hot debate ever since

Figure 11. Stela 1, El Baúl

its finding in 1923, some refusing to believe it even as old as the Classic Period, and its very discoverer claiming it as Aztec! On the right, a profile figure is stiffly posed with spear in hand below a cloud-scroll; over the lower part of his face is some sort of covering, while to his head-dress is attached a chin strap, a feature known to be extremely early in the Maya lowlands. In front of him are two vertical columns of glyphs, the right-hand of which consists of little more than empty cartouches which probably were meant to be painted. Let us however consider the row on the extreme left, for this is almost surely the earliest dated monument in the Maya area proper. At the top is the coefficient twelve above a fleshless jaw, a Mexican form of the day sign Eb. Then there are four undecipherable signs, followed by a series of Long Count numbers which can be reconstructed as 7.19.15.7.12, reaching the Calendar Round position 12 Eb; in terms of our own calendar, this would be A.D. 36, some 256 years prior to the first such date in the Maya lowlands, but significantly later than the precocious inscriptions of Chiapas and the Veracruz coast.

We cannot leave the Pacific coastal zone without mentioning a second sculptural tradition which reaches some degree of popularity both there and at Kaminaljuyú. This is expressed in large, crude, pot-bellied statues with puffy faces and lower jaws so inflated that they have been compared with the late Il Duce of Italy. At Monte Alto, not far from El Baúl, a group of these monstrous forms is placed in a row along with a colossal head (plate 6) carried out in the same style, and some believe that the entire pot-bellied complex is connected with the Olmec culture and precedes the Izapan. However, since Monte Alto is strewn with Late Formative pottery sherds, it is most likely that this was a subsidiary cult that coexisted with the Izapan Rain God, just as Egyptian and Greco-Roman religious art flourished side by side in ancient Alexandria. But a cult to what deity? A fairly good case can be made out for this being none other than the Fat God, without known functions but ubiquitous among the peoples of Mexico and the Northern Maya Area in Classic times.

Kaminaljuyú and the Maya Highlands

A Late Formative rival to Izapa in size and number of temple mounds and in the splendour of its carved monuments was Kaminaljuyú (figure 12) during the Miraflores phase. This, it

Figure 12. View of Kaminaljuyú, looking west, from a photograph taken by A. P. Maudslay. Most of the earthen mounds are temple substructures of the Miraflores culture

will be recalled, was once a major ceremonial site on the western outskirts of Guatemala City. The majority of the approximately 200 mounds once to be found there were probably thrown up by the Miraflores people, whose rulers must have possessed a formidable economic and political power over much of the Maya highlands at this time.

The excavation of two Miraflores tombs has thrown much

light on the luxury to which these rulers were accustomed. Mound E-III-3 (figure 13) at Kaminaljuyú consists of several superimposed temple platforms, each a flat-topped, stepped pyramid fronted by a broad stairway; in its final form it reaches a height of more than sixty feet. In lieu of easily worked building stone, which was unavailable in the vicinity, these platforms were built from ordinary clay and basketloads of earth and household rubbish. Almost certainly the temples themselves were thatched-roof affairs supported by upright timbers. Apparently each successive building operation took place to house the remains of an exalted person, whose tomb was cut down from the top in a series of stepped rectangles of decreasing size into the earlier temple platform, and then covered over with a new floor of clay. The function of Maya pyramids as funerary monuments thus harks back to Pre-Classic times.

The corpse was wrapped in finery and covered from head to toe with cinnabar pigment, then laid on a wooden litter and lowered into the tomb. Both sacrificed adults and children accompanied the illustrious dead, along with offerings of an astonishing richness and profusion. In one tomb over 300 objects of the most beautiful workmanship were placed in with the body or above the timber roof, but ancient grave-robbers, probably acting after noticing the slump in the temple floor caused by the collapse of the underlying tomb, had filched from the corpse the jades which once covered chest and head. Among the finery recovered were the remains of a mask or head-dress of jade plaques perhaps once fixed to a background of wood, jade flares which once adorned the ear lobes of the honoured dead, bowls carved from chlorite-schist (plate 7) engraved with Miraflores scroll designs, and little carved bottles of soapstone (plate 10) and fuchsite.

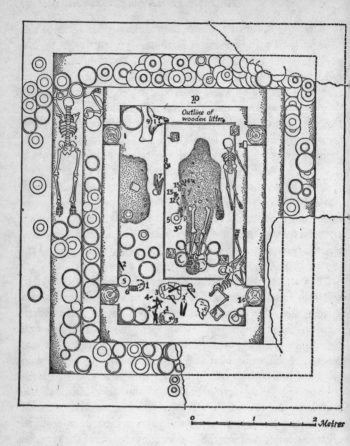

Figure 13. Plan of Tomb II, Mound E–III–3, a burial of the Miraflores culture at Kaminaljuyú. 1, jade beads; 2, obsidian flake-blades; 3, mica sheets; 4, jade mosaic element; 5, stuccoed gourds; 6, pebbles; 7, basalt implements; 8, human teeth; 9, jade mosaic mask or head-dress; 10, obsidian stones; 11, pyrite-incrusted sherd; 12, soapstone implement; 13, bone objects, fish teeth, and quartz crystals; 14, sting-ray spines; 15, spatulate bone object. All other circular objects are pottery vessels

Miraflores pottery vessels from E-III-3 (plate 9) and elsewhere belong to a ceramic tradition prevalent throughout south-eastern Mesoamerica during the Late Formative horizon, from Izapa to El Salvador, and up into the Central and Northern Maya area, but are set off from this in their refinement and sophistication. Shapes have now become exuberant, with re-curved outlines, elaborate flanges on rims and bodies, and the appearance of vessel feet. Some of the most amusing examples of the potter's art are effigy vessels, a few of which show smiling old men. Painted stucco is often used to achieve effects in colours such as pink and green, unobtainable in fired slips. Most bowls and jars are embellished with engraved and carved scroll designs. A more peculiar kind of decoration which is virtually a marker for the Late Formative Period in the Maya area is Usulután (cf. plate 14), believed to originate in El Salvador where it attains great popularity. On this widely traded ware a resistant substance such as wax or a thin clay was applied to bowls with a multiple-brush applicator; after smudging or darkening in a reducing fire, the material was removed to leave a design of wavy, parallel, yellowish lines on a darker orange or brown background.

As for stone carving on a larger scale, it was once believed that the Miraflores people made only 'mushroom stones'. These peculiar objects, one of which was found in an E-III-3 tomb, are of unknown use. Some see vaguely phallic associations. Others, such as Dr Borhegyi, connect them with the cult of the hallucinogenic mushrooms still to this day prevalent in the Mexican highlands, and it is claimed that the mortars and pestles with which the stones are so often found associated were used in the preparatory rites.

But we have much more to go by than that, thanks to the devastation of Kaminaljuyú by modern real-estate entrepreneurs. It now appears that there were Miraflores artists capable of creating sculpture on a large scale, in an Izapan style that can only be called the forerunner of the Classic Maya. Moreover, the élite of this valley were fully literate at a time when other Maya were perhaps just learning that writing existed. Two of these monuments were encountered by accident in a drainage ditch. One is a tall, granite stela embellished with a striding figure (plate 11) wearing a series of grotesque masks of the Izapan Long-lipped God, and carrying a chipped flint of eccentric form in one hand. On either side of him are spiked clay incense burners exactly like those found in Miraflores excavations. The other (figure 14) is even more extraordinary. It must have been of gigantic proportions before its deliberate breakage; the surviving fragments show that there were several Izapan gods, one bearded, surrounding a human figure with downpointing tridents in place of eyes, probably a precursor of a god who later appears at Tikal (plate 22); he too, wields an eccentric flint. The glyphs associated with these figures may be their calendric names, for in ancient Meso-america both gods and men were identified by the days on which they were born. A much longer text in several columns is incised below in a script which is otherwise unknown but which, in the opinion of Miss Proskouriakoff and others, may foreshadow Classic Maya writing, since there are strong simil-arities in form if not in specific characters. It cannot, however, yet be read.

Not only were stelae of major size carved by the Miraflores artisans, but also tenoned figures called 'silhouette sculptures', which were perhaps originally meant to be stuck upright into temple and plaza floors; frog- or toad-effigy figures of all sizes; and many other forms. Once more, the pot-bellied figures are ubiquitous: did they represent a cult of the people, separate from the more aristocratic religion of the rulers? Or do they, as some believe, belong to an earlier horizon?

Figure 14. Broken Miraflores stela from Kaminaljuyú

Archaeology has unfortunately arrived on the scene too late to answer this.

The astonishing wealth of the Miraflores people, their artistic and architectural capabilities, their obvious relation to the Classic Maya in matters of style, iconography, and script – all these things lead one to believe that the Izapan culture of the highlands must have had a good deal to do with the adoption of civilized life in the Central and Northern Areas. While the pre-eminence of Kaminaljuyú during the Late Formative period is plain to see, its star began to sink by the second and third centuries A.D., and most of it was left in ruin within the brief century or two of the Proto-Classic. It is not until the Mexican invasions of the Early Classic that this great centre regains its former splendour.

The Petén and the Maya Lowlands

While the Maya highlands and Pacific Coast were experiencing an extraordinary cultural efflorescence in the Late Formative, the Central and Northern Areas were hardly slumbering. Within the boundless forests the agricultural economy and society had advanced to such a degree that massive temple centres were already rising in jungle clearings. But it is clear that from the very beginning the people of the lowlands were taking a somewhat different course from that of their kinsmen to the south, and it is their unique qualities which so distinguished them in the Classic period which was soon to be inaugurated.

Although there are minor differences from region to region, a single widespread culture, Chicanel, dominated the Central and Northern Areas at this time. Usulután ware (plate 14) and vessels with widely everted lips, elaborate rim flanges, or complex outline are, as in the Southern Area, hallmarks for the period. Most pottery is legless, and confined to a simple black or red monochrome, with thick glossy slips that feel waxy to the touch. It is strange that in most known Chicanel sites, figurines are not found, from which it may be supposed that there was a change in popular cults.

The most unusual feature of Chicanel culture, however, is the high elaboration of architecture, above all in the latter part of the Late Formative, from 100 B.C. to A.D. 150. It must be remembered that the Petén-Yucatán shelf is blessed with an in-exhaustible supply of easily cut limestone, and with abundant flint for tools with which to work it. Moreover, the Maya of the lowlands had discovered as far back as Mamom times that if limestone fragments were burnt, and the resulting powder mixed with water, a white plaster of great durability was obtained. And finally, they quickly realized the structural value of a concrete-like fill made from limestone rubble and marl.

With these resources at hand, the Maya temple architect was able to create some elaborate constructions at a very early date. At the great Petén sites of Uaxactún and Tikal deep excavations have shown that major pyramids, platforms and courts were already taking shape by the late Chicanel times. There is general agreement, for instance, that the E-VII-sub pyramid (plate 8) at Uaxactún was built late in the Chicanel phase; beautifully preserved by the overlay of later structures, this truncated temple platform is faced by brilliantly white plaster and rises in several tiers each having the apron mould-ings which are so distinctive a feature of Maya architecture in the lowlands. On all four sides are centrally placed, inset stairways flanked by great monster masks which some see as derived from the old Olmec Rain God, although certain of them more probably represent sky-serpents. Post-holes sunk into the floor show that the superstructure was a building of pole and thatch.

Even more advanced temples have been uncovered at Tikal, which lies only a half-day's walk south of Uaxactún. Two late Chicanel structures, for instance, had superstructures with masonry walls, and it is possible, though certainly not proved, that the rooms were spanned by the corbel vault, or so-called 'false arch'. Some quite extraordinary paintings embellished the outer walls of one of these temples, showing human figures standing in a background of cloud-like scrolls, carried out by a sure hand in black, yellow, red, and pink. Another set of murals, this time in black on a red background, was found inside a late Chicanel burial chamber at Tikal. The subject matter comprises six richly attired figures, probably both human and divine. The two sets, which are thought to date from the last half of the first century B.C., are pretty clearly in the Izapan style characteristic of Kaminaljuyú.

Some of the Late Formative tombs at Tikal prove that the Chicanel élite did not lag behind the nobles of Miraflores in wealth and honour. Burial 85, for instance, like all the others enclosed by platform substructures and covered by a primitive corbel vault, contained a single skeleton. Surprisingly, this individual lacked head and thigh bones, but from the richness of the goods placed with him it may be guessed that he must have perished in battle and been despoiled by his enemies, his mutilated body being later recovered by his subjects. The remains were carefully wrapped up in textiles, and the bundle placed in an upright position. A small, greenstone mask (plate 12) with shell-inlaid eyes and teeth seems to have been sewn to the bundle to represent the head. A sting-ray spine, the symbol of self-sacrifice among the Maya, and a spondylus shell were added to the gruesome contents. Packed around the burial chamber were no less than twenty-six vessels of the late Chicanel period, (plate 14) one of which contained pine-wood charcoal dated by the radiocarbon process to A.D. 16 ± 131.

Such Late Formative splendour is found throughout the lowlands wherever the spade has gone deep enough. Even in the seemingly less favourable Northern Area, there are enormous constructions datable to this era, such as the great high mound at Yaxuná, a temple substructure having a ground plan of sixty by 130 metres.

By the Proto-Classic of the second and third centuries A.D. we are on the threshold of Classic Maya civilization. Temples arranged around plazas, construction with limestone and plaster, apron mouldings and frontal stairways on pyramids, tomb building, and frescoes with naturalistic subjects – all had already taken shape by the end of the Late Formative. The brief Proto-Classic epoch sees the intrusion of new ceramic traits which seem to have been first elaborated in British Honduras; the most important of these are the addition of hollow, breast-shaped supports to bowls, hour-glass-shaped pot-stands, and polychrome. Maya polychrome is distinguished by a brilliant range of colours applied over a glossy, translucent orange underslip, but wherever it was first invented it certainly was not native to the Petén region. Corbelling of rooms must have evolved from methods employed in the construction of tombs, and by A.D. 250 began to be in universal use at Petén sites. The principle is simple (cf. figure 25): above the springline of the walls, successive courses of stones were set in overlapping rows up to the vault summit (plate 38), which was capped by flat stones. However, there is an inherent structural weakness, and the great thrust from above is taken up in Maya buildings by massive walls and by the strength of the rubble-cement fill. Nevertheless, once adopted, it became the badge of Maya architecture in the lowlands, as opposed to the thatched- or flat-beam roofs of Mexico.

The list is impressive, and one would think on the face of it that Maya civilization had emerged independently here in the lowlands, several centuries before the opening of the Classic era. But two items are missing or exceedingly rare: monuments with Long Count dates, and writing. These we know were present among the coeval Izapan centres of the highlands and Pacific Coast, and it is probable that they were derived from the even older Olmec civilization of the Gulf Coast. The Izapan style was spread from outside into the Central and Northern areas—a broken carving from a Proto-Classic level of the Tikal acropolis, the early Tikal frescoes, and a human figure on the walls of Loltun cave in Yucatán all testify to this – but literacy and a concern with recording dates did not become prevalent in the lowlands until the eve of the Classic Period.

[4] Classic Splendour: The Early Period

During a span of six centuries, from about A.D. 300 to 900, the Maya, particularly those of the Central Area, reached intellectual and artistic heights which no others in the New World, and few in the Old, could match at that time. The Classic Period (figure 15) was a kind of golden age, not only for them but for the rest of the. Mesoamerican peoples. Large populations, an abundant economy, and widespread trade were typical of the Classic, but although it was once thought to have been a period of relative peace and tranquillity in comparison to what followed, that notion has in the main been disproved. It is an equally unfounded assumption that the Classic peoples were ruled by priests. On the contrary, we shall see that the ancient Maya were just as warlike and had as thoroughly secular a government as the supposedly more bloodthirsty states of the Post-Classic.

The Classic can only be defined accurately as that span during which the lowland Maya were using the Long Count calendar on their monuments. In 1864 workmen engaged in digging a canal near Puerto Barrios, on the steamy Caribbean coast of Guatemala, came across a jade plaque which subsequently found its way to Leiden, Holland. The Leiden Plate (figure 16) has engraved on one face a richly bedecked Maya lord, trampling underfoot a sorry-looking captive, a theme repeated on so many Maya stelae of later times. On the other side is inscribed the Long Count date 8.14.3.1.12, corresponding

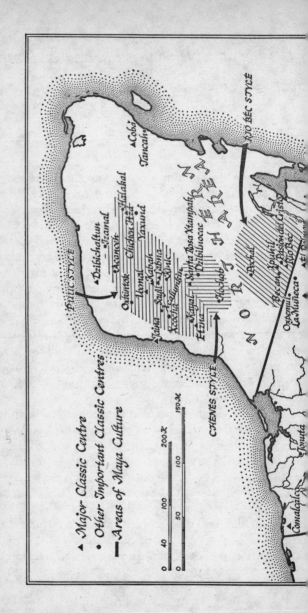

- ▲ *Major Classic Centre*
- • *Other Important Classic Centres*
- ➔ *Areas of Maya Culture*

Figure 15. Sites of the Classic Period

to A.D. 320. The style of the glyphs and the costume and pose of the person depicted call to mind the Late Formative monuments of the highlands and Pacific Coast, but in this

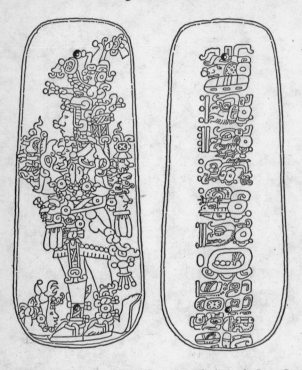

Figure 16. The Leiden Plate. The reverse side carries the Long Count date 8.14.3.1.12, corresponding to A.D. 320 Height 8½ in.

case the date is preceded by the typical Maya Introductory Glyph, and the bar-and-dot numbers are followed by the signs for baktun and lesser periods. Until recently the Leiden Plate was considered the most ancient object dated in Maya fashion, but now we have Stela 29 from Tikal, erected 28 years before, in 8.12.14.8.15 (A.D. 292).

Thus the lowland Maya had definitely received the Long Count by the close of the third century A.D. From this event until the Classic downfall, we have a very closely dated archaeological sequence governed by the carving of stelae and other monuments, which themselves have been tied at Uaxactún and other sites with the construction of floors, building stages, and tombs. The Classic very conveniently divides itself into an Early and a Late Period at about A.D. 600; however, this division is not merely an invention of the archaeologist, for not only did a profound upheaval take place in the Central Area at that time, but there are considerable cultural differences between the two halves.

Two things set off the Early from the Late Classic: firstly, the strong Izapan element still discernible in Maya culture, and secondly, the appearance in the latter part of the Early Classic of powerful waves of influence from the site of Teotihuacán in central Mexico. This city was founded at about the time of Christ in a small but fertile valley opening onto the north-east side of the Valley of Mexico itself. On the eve of its destruction at the hands of unknown peoples, at the end of the sixth century A.D., it covered an area of over eight square miles. Teotihuacán is noted for the regularity of its great avenues, for its Pyramids of the Sun and Moon, and for the delicacy and sophistication of the wall paintings which graced the walls of its luxurious palaces. So mighty was the city that it held dominion over most of Mexico in the Early Classic, as the centre of an empire which may well have been greater than that of the much later Aztec. From what economic base such political and cultural power derived is unclear, but it may have been linked to adoption of the unique and incredibly productive system of *chinampa* cultivation carried out by draining and cultivating the swampy margins of the Great Lake which then filled the Valley of Mexico. This was the city which interfered in such a significant way with the course of Maya history.

The Esperanza Culture

The disintegration of Maya culture in the highlands began with the close of the Miraflores period, when building activity slackens at major sites. In fact, by the end of the Proto-Classic the great ceremonial centre of Kaminaljuyú, focal point of Maya cultural and political affairs in the Southern Area, appears to have been a virtual ruin.

Shortly after A.D. 400 the highlands fell under Teotihuacán domination. An intrusive group of central Mexicans from that city seized Kaminaljuyú and built for themselves a miniature version of their capital. An élite class ruling over a captive population of Maya descent, they were swayed by native cultural tastes and traditions and were influenced by the Maya to the extent that they imported from the Central Area pottery and other wares with which to stock their tombs. The Esperanza culture which arose at Kaminaljuyú during the Early Classic, then, is a kind of hybrid.

There are several complexes of Esperanza architecture at Kaminaljuyú, all built on a plan which is not in the least bit Maya. Essentially these are stepped temple platforms (figure 17) with the typical Teotihuacán *talud-tablero* motif, in which a rectangular panel with inset is placed over a sloping batter (*talud*). The good building stone which is so abundant in the Mexican highlands is missing at Kaminaljuyú, so that the architect, almost certainly a Teotihuacano himself, had to be content with clay, faced with red-painted stucco. A single stairway fronted each stage of the platform, while on top a temple sanctuary was roofed either with thatch or with the more usual flat beam-and-mortar construction of Teotihuacán.

The foreign lords of the Esperanza phase chose the temple platforms themselves as their final resting places. As with the earlier Miraflores people, each platform was actually built to

Figure 17. Structure A-7, Kaminaljuyú, a temple-pyramid of the Esperanza culture

enclose the ruler's tomb, a log-roofed chamber usually placed beneath the frontal staircase, successive burials and their platforms being placed over older ones. The honoured deceased was buried in a seated posture upon a wooden bier and was accompanied to the other world not only by rich offerings of pottery and other artifacts, but also by one to three persons sacrificed for the occasion, generally children or adolescents. Surrounding him were rich funerary vessels, undoubtedly containing food and drink for his own use, as well as implements such as *metates* and *manos* needed to prepare them.

Jade ornaments (plate 18), some in the process of manufacture, were recovered in quantity from the Esperanza tombs: beads, complex ear ornaments in the form of flared spools, pendants, and spangles are ubiquitous. Underneath one staircase was found a 200 lb. boulder of jade from which V-shaped slices had been sawn, indicating that the Esperanza élite had access to a major source of this substance so precious to all the peoples of Mesoamerica.

Few of the pottery vessels from the Esperanza tombs are represented in the rubbish strewn around Kaminaljuyú, from which it is clear that they were intended for the use of the invading class alone. Some of these were actually imported from Teotihuacán itself, probably carried laboriously over the intervening eight or nine hundred miles on back racks such as those still used by Indian traders in the Maya highlands. The ceramic hallmarks of the Teotihuacán civilization are the cylindrical vessels with three slab feet and cover (plate 13); a little jug with open spout and handle; the '*florero*', so called from its resemblance to a small flower-vase; and Thin Orange ware (plate 15), made to Teotihuacán taste in northern Puebla. All are present in Esperanza, but so are polychrome bowls (cf. figure 18) from the Petén, with their peculiar 'basal flanges'.

Certain of the tripod vessels have been stuccoed and painted in brilliant colours with feather-bedecked Teotihuacán lords, or seated Maya personages and both Maya and Teotihuacán deities, including the Butterfly Goddess so popular in Mexico. One Petén Maya polychrome bowl had even been overpainted with processional figures in Teotihuacán style, speech scrolls curling from their mouths.

All sorts of other valuables were placed with the dead. That Esperanza pomp, perhaps the funeral itself, was accompanied by music is shown by shell trumpets and by large turtle carapaces used with deer-antler beaters as percussive instruments. On a large effigy incense burner from one grave, a seated person strikes a two-toned slit drum. Besides jade, the corpse was ornamented with pearls, cut-out pieces of mica, and rich textiles which have long since rotted away. Included in several tombs were pairs of jaguar paws, symbols of royal power among the highland Maya. The highest technical achievement is seen in the mirrors made up of pyrite plates cut into polygonal shapes and fitted to each other over a circular disk of slate. These are in all likelihood another import from Teotihuacán, but the back of one proved to have remarkable carving in an elaborate scrollwork style that is associated with the Classic Veracruz civilization then developing on the Gulf Coast of Mexico. The ability of the Esperanza rulers to amass luxurious objects from the most distant parts must have been considerable.

The Esperanza culture may have its spectacular side, but almost as striking are the omissions. The Long Count calendar had disappeared from the Southern Maya Area for good, which is strange considering its ancient roots here. The figurine cult had utterly disappeared. Nor is there any sure indication of stone sculpture on any scale in Esperanza Kaminaljuyú. The evolution of Maya culture in the Southern Area, especially in the highlands, had come to a very abrupt end with the establishment of Teotihuacán hegemony, and apart from the imports of Petén products, Maya ways of doing things were replaced with Mexican from the Early Classic on. Were these intruders warriors or traders? They may well have been both. By Aztec times in central Mexico there was a special caste of armed merchants called *pochteca*, who journeyed into distant countries in search of rare manufactures and raw materials not available in the homeland, all of which were destined for the king. From representations of the *pochteca* god at Teotihuacán, we know that the institution is at least as old as the Early Classic. Thus, Kaminaljuyú may have been a south-easterly outpost of long-distance traders from that great city, established for the purpose of exporting Maya riches for the Teotihuacán throne. As will be seen, the presence of this foreign group was felt through the Petén and as far north as Yucatán itself.

As for the vanquished Maya of the Guatemalan highlands, they must have continued on as before, rendering tribute to Mexican rather than native overlords, tillers of the land and labourers on public construction projects. The great public ceremonials of Kaminaljuyú may even have been forbidden to them. But one cult in which they were certainly allowed to participate was centred upon Lake Amatitlán, not far south of the Esperanza capital, where hot springs and fumaroles along the southern shore must have attracted annual processions rendering homage to the gods of water and fire. Skin-divers have brought up many hundreds of blackened vessels from the hot mud of the lake bottom, ranging from extraordinary incense burners (plate 29) to the pots and pans of the peasant household, all cast by devotees into the steaming waters.

Tzakol Culture in the Central Area

Early Classic remains in the Central Area are burdened with towering constructions of Late Classic date, and it has only been quite recently that the elaboration of Maya civilization during this period has been fully realized. The Tzakol culture, as the civilization of the Petén and surrounding regions is called, endures until about 9.8.0.0.0 or, to round it off in Christian years, until A.D. 600.

Already Maya civilization is in full flower, with enormous

ceremonial centres crowded with masonry temples and 'palaces' facing onto spacious plazas covered with white stucco. Stelae and altars are carved with dates and embellished with the figures of men and perhaps gods. Polychrome pottery (figure 18), the finest examples of which were sealed up in the tombs of honoured personages, emphasizes stylized polychrome designs of cranes, flying parrots, or men, often on bowls with a kind of apron or basal flange encircling the lower part. Along with these purely Maya ceramics are vessels (cf. plate 23) which show the imprint of distant Teotihuacán: again, the cylindrical vase supported by three slab legs, the small, spouted jug and the *florero*.

The wonderful Maya mural art has its roots in the Chicanel wall paintings of Tikal, but by Tzakol times it has reached a very high degree of elaboration. Now mutilated by local vandals, the lovely Early Classic wall paintings of Temple B-XIII at Uaxactún were executed in muted tones of red, brown, tan, and black. The scene is one from real life: before a palace building sheltering three Maya ladies, two male figures, one painted a warlike black, are in conversation (which is undoubtedly recorded in several columns of undecipherable glyphs). At one side are two horizontal rows of figures, probably meant as standing on two levels of a stepped platform, painted with a strong feeling for individual caricature; a few are chattering in excited discourse. Some are singers shaking rattles, while a small boy beats time on a skin-covered drum.

Burials of great richness have been uncovered beneath Tzakol temples in several Petén sites. Among the most striking is the 'Painted Tomb' chamber (plate 17), nine feet long by five feet wide, cut from the soft bedrock underlying an Early Classic temple facing the Great Plaza at Tikal. There were three interments here, two of them adolescent victims

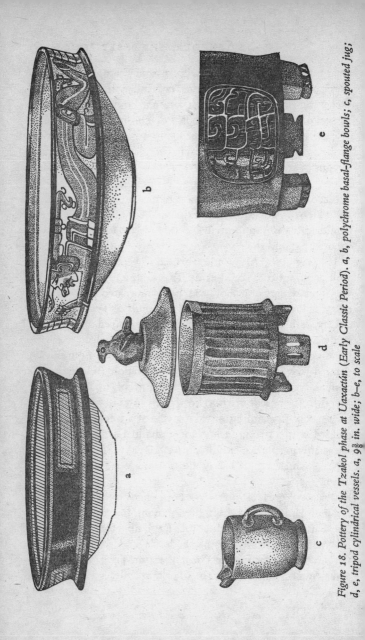

Figure 18. Pottery of the Tzakol phase at Uaxactún (Early Classic Period). a, b, polychrome basal-flange bowls; c, spouted jug; d, e, tripod cylindrical vessels. a, 9⅜ in. wide; b–e, to scale

sacrificed to accompany the principal personage, a headless and handless corpse presumably recovered by his followers from the scene of a military disaster. The white, stuccoed walls had been covered with glyphs applied in black paint by a sure hand, including the Long Count date 9.1.1.10.10 (18 March, A.D. 457), in all likelihood the day of the man's death or of his funeral. A *metate* and *mano*, and vessels once filled with food (one had contained some pigeon-sized birds) show that the soul was to be nourished in the after-life. Marine shells and sting-ray spines, imported from distant shores, were placed with the dead. Besides pottery vessels, the tomb contained an alabaster pedestal bowl encircled by a row of incised glyphs, the lines of which were filled with red cinnabar.

Although influence from Teotihuacán, or from its Kaminal-juyú outpost, has for some time been suspected for the Central Area during the Early Classic, the full extent of this has only begun to become clear through recent excavations at Tikal, in the very heart of the Petén. It is also apparent that the foreign impact is strongest at about A.D. 500, in the last century of the Early Classic.

Stela 31 (plate 19) from Tikal, apparently erected at this time, hints at the nature of this influence, and would tell us more if only we could read its finely carved Maya text. The principal figure of the relief is a great Maya personage, loaded down with jade ornaments almost to the point of obscuring him, who carries in the crook of his left arm the head of a god wearing in its head-dress the Tikal 'Emblem Glyph' (cf. figure 49a) (see chapter 8). On either side is a standing warrior whose dress and armament (rectangular shield and *atlatl*, or spear-thrower) brands him as a foreigner from Teotihuacán. One of the shields shows the face of the great Teotihuacán Rain God, Tlaloc. Was Tikal like Kaminaljuyú, a suzerainty of Teotihuacán? Or were those foreign mercenaries in the employ of a native king? The city-dwellers of Teotihuacán were a mercantile people, and it would have been greatly in the interest of an armed *pochteca* group to have seized the Petén so as to control the commerce originating in the Maya jungles. Perhaps it was the resplendent, gold-green tail feathers of the shy quetzal that they were seeking, to adorn the head-dresses of Teohituacán nobles.

They might also have tried to impose the worship of Teo-tihuacán gods upon the Petén Maya, substituting their own rain god for the native Chac. To this the upper part of a shattered stela from Tikal (figure 19), showing a large Tlaloc face exactly like that upon the shield of Stela 31, is testimony. On finely stuccoed and painted vessels from the Tikal tombs is the blue-faced Tlaloc again, along with the Mexican god of spring, Xipe Totec (plate 16), recognized by the open mouth and the pairs of vertical lines which pass through the eyes across the cheeks. Some of these vessels are Thin Orange ware manufactured in the Mexican highlands, another comes from the Tiquisate region on the Pacific Coast of Guatemala, while others represent hybrids in shape and decoration between Maya and Teotihuacán traditions.

There almost certainly was a heavy trade between the Petén and the Valley of Mexico. Tzakol sherds from basal flange bowls have been found at Teotihuacán, and green obsidian blades from central Mexico were placed with the Tikal dead. However, of all the perishable products which must have travelled the same routes – textiles, quetzal feathers, jaguar pelts, wooden objects, and so forth – nothing remains.

Not only in the northern Petén, but at many other places in the Central Area, major Maya centres (cf. plates 20, 24, 25) were well established by the sixth century A.D. and even earlier. At these, Teotihuacán domination is less easy, or even impossible, to demonstrate, and one can suppose that this was

Figure 19. Fragmentary stela in Teotihuacán style from Tikal

restricted to the Tikal-Uaxactún area alone. Whatever might be the nature of Teotihuacán in the affairs, both political and cultural, of the Petén Maya, in the last half of the sixth century a serious crisis shook the Central Area. No more stelae were erected, and there is indication of widespread and purposeful mutilation of public monuments. It is not clear what all this means, but although none of the Petén sites actually seems to have been abandoned near the close of the Early Classic, there might have been a fierce internecine warfare or perhaps even a popular revolt.

When the smoke clears, in the first decades of the seventh century, Classic Maya life is seen to have been reconstituted much as before, possibly with new rulers and new dynasties. But Teotihuacán is no longer a factor in Maya civilization. In some great event of which we have no written record, that city was destroyed, and the empire of which it was the capital came to an end. This took place by A.D. 600, and probably was the decisive factor resulting in the Maya disturbances in the closing decades of the Early Classic. However, the release from a foreign yoke which was economic and probably also political enabled the lowland Maya of the Central Area to reach unparalleled heights in the Late Classic Period.

The Northern Area

A good deal less is known about the Early Classic in the stony land of Yucatán and Campeche than in the south. In both ceramics (plate 23) and architecture these Maya closely adhered to Petén standards. One of the earliest centres is Oxkintok in the scrubby plain of western Yucatán, with a stone lintel carved in the fifth century A.D., and some contemporary but aesthetically inferior reliefs.

A more interesting site is Acanceh, south-east of Mérida, the present-day capital of Yucatán. On the one hand, there is a stepped pyramid-platform with inset stairway of apron mouldings of straightforward Petén Maya type. On the other, there is an extraordinary platform with a *talud-tablero* façade (plate 27), stuccoed with relief figures in Teotihuacán style: anthropomorphic bats, birds of prey, a squirrel, and a representation of the central deity of Teotihuacán, known as the Feathered Serpent or Quetzalcóatl. There is nothing Maya about this building. On the contrary, it is evidence that the dynamic people of Teotihuacán had established outposts not only in the Southern and Central Areas, but also here in the Northern Area, foreshadowing the great Mexican invasions that were to take place in Yucatán five centuries later.

The Cotzumalhuapa Problem

The Pipil have always been an enigmatic people. Their language (figure 2) is Náhuat, a close relative of Náhuatl, the official tongue of the Aztec, differing mainly from the latter by a substitution of *t* in place of *tl*. Having intruded into the Maya area at some unknown time from an equally unknown region in Mexico, by the Spanish Conquest the Pipil had established a major settlement in a small zone within the well-watered piedmont zone just above the Pacific plain of Guatemala. From traditions recorded in colonial times, however, it is known that their domain had once extended somewhat to the west into lands later claimed by the Cakchiquel Maya.

This once-Pipil territory is the locus of a vanished civilization which was indisputably Mexican, centring upon the town of Santa Lucía Cotzumalhuapa, in a region which once was famed for its production of cacao, the chocolate beans used not only for drink but as currency. There are only about a half-dozen Cotzumalhuapan sites known, or perhaps just one large one, for all lie within a tiny area of only twenty square miles. Each is a compact ceremonial centre consisting of temple substructures arranged on a single large platform measuring only a few hundred yards on its long axis; structures have earthen cores faced with river cobbles, but stairways and some courts were occasionally covered with dressed stone.

From the evidence of art style and pottery the Cotzumalhuapan culture must have arisen in the latter part of the Early Classic, and endured into the Late. A more hard, cruel, and unsympathetic sculptural style could hardly be imagined (plate 26), or one less Maya in its general aspect. As Eric Thompson notes, the Cotzumalhuapan sculptors showed 'a haunting preoccupation with death'. Reliefs of skulls and manikin figures of skeletons are not uncommon. Their second obsession was the rubber-ball game. Secure evidence for the game comes from certain stone objects which are frequent in the Cotzumalhuapan zone and in fact over much of the Pacific coast down to El Salvador. Of these, most typical are the U-shaped stone 'yokes', which represented the heavy protective belts of wood and leather worn by the contestants; and thin heads or *hachas* (plate 28) with human faces, grotesque carnivores, macaws, and turkeys, generally thought to be markers for the zones of the court, but worn on the yoke during post-game ceremonies. Both are sure signs of a close affiliation to the Classic cultures of the Mexican Gulf Coast, where such ball-game paraphernalia undoubtedly originated.

Among the relief and in-the-round sculptures of the Cotzumalhuapan sites are representations of some purely Mexican gods: Xipe Totec; the Wind God Ehécatl, shown as a horrifically snouted monster with one extruded eyeball; Tlaloc; Tlalchitonatíuh, god of the rising sun; the Old Fire God, Huehuetéotl; and Quetzalcóatl as Feathered Serpent. On some magnificent stelae ball players wearing 'yokes' and protective gloves (figure 20) reach up to celestial deities, usually the Sun or Moon. From the bodies of gods and men may sprout the fronds and pods of cacao, the apparent source of Cotzumalhuapan wealth.

Not only their religion, but their very calendar was Mexican. The majority of the glyphs on the monuments are recognizable as the kind of day-names prevalent among the peoples of southern Mexico, while the numbers of the coefficients are expressed in the Mexican fashion by dots or circles only,

Figure 20. Monument 4 from Santa Lucía Cotzumalhuapa. Cotzumalhuapa culture, end of the Early Classic or beginning of the Late Classic

without the use of the bar for 'five' so characteristic of the Maya. Again, as in Mexico, individuals (and perhaps gods, too) were identified by the day of their birth.

The creators of the Cotzumalhuapan civilization, then, were not Mayan but Mexican, most likely the Pipil themselves.

Yet, while some of their art and a few of their pottery vessels can be related to Teotihuacán, they could not have come from that city. There are surer connections with the Gulf Coast plain, where there is a similar concentration upon the ball game, death, human sacrifice, and the cultivation of cacao. If these were the Pipil, then there might have been an ancient centre of Náhuat speakers in southern Veracruz who, as another *pochteca* group, could have invaded the southern Maya area across the Isthmus of Tehuantepec. It will be recalled that there is a further enclave of Pipil on the other side of the highlands in the Motagua Valley of Guatemala, and it is probably no accident that isolated sculptures in Cotzumalhuapan style have been found there at Quiriguá and at near-by Copán, both otherwise purely Classic Maya centres. But the Cotzumalhuapa problem is very far from solved.

[5] Classic Splendour: The Late Period

The great culture of the Maya lowlands during the Late Classic period is one of the 'lost' civilizations of the world, its hundreds of ceremonial centres buried under an almost unbroken canopy of tropical forest. We would like to know who lived in these now-decayed centres, how large the lowland Maya population really was in the Late Classic, and how the Maya realm was then governed. This, however, we do know: that none of the great sites which are often called 'cities' were anything of the sort.

Large masonry buildings are easy to map, but, curiously enough, so are the simple huts of the common people, for the ancient Maya conveniently raised their houses on low rectangular mounds of earth and stone to avoid the summer floods. In a survey of the north-eastern Petén, which includes such enormous Classic centres as Tikal, Naranjo, Nakum, and Holmul, Dr William Bullard found that the density of house ruins had very little to do with these sites; but house mounds rather tended to be clustered along ridges where drinking water and rich, well-drained soils were close at hand. The bulk of the people lived in unplanned hamlets roughly 200 to 300 yards square, separated from other settlements by terrain features such as the *bajos* which are such a characteristic feature of the Petén, or by savannahs. The houses were of pole and thatch, often in compounds like the patriarchal dwellings of the Chinese peasant. Sometimes one of the houses of the hamlet is larger than the others and can be interpreted as a small shrine or communal building for the local farmers.

For every 50 to 100 dwellings in the Central Area, there is a minor ceremonial centre, this with its dependent clusters making up what Bullard calls a 'zone'. One has to think of a dispersed population corresponding in some ways to our township with the minor centre, usually comprising a small temple pyramid and several palace-like buildings, serving as a focus for religious and civic activities. Because of the amorphous nature of Maya settlement – there were no real town plans, no checkerboard of neatly planned streets – there sometimes is no clear break between zones, so that some unwary archaeologists in the lowlands, stumbling on ruins extending for many miles, have imagined that they have discovered the biggest site in the world.

Major ceremonial centres, such as Uaxactún, Tikal, or Palenque in the Central Area, or Uxmal in the Northern, were nuclei for 'districts' subdivided into zones. Bullard calculates that on the average the area of a district was something less than 100 square kilometres, and compares it to a modern county or province. Tikal (figure 21) is the largest of all Maya sites and the only one that has been completely mapped down to the last house mound, although in view of the difficulty of drawing boundaries around any settlement of the lowlands it is hard to say exactly where it ends. Within a little over six square miles there are about 3,000 structures, ranging from lofty temple pyramids and massive palaces to tiny household units of thatch-roofed huts. A very reasonable estimate of the total Tikal population in Late Classic times is about 10,000 to 11,000 persons. This is equivalent to a density of approximately 1,700 persons per square mile, as compared with the more than 5,000 per square mile of an average city in modern Europe or America. A glance at the Tikal layout will show

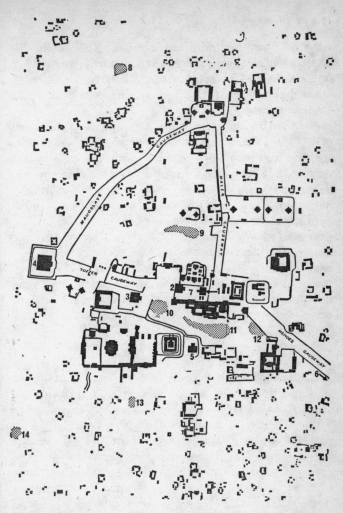

Figure 21. Plan of the central part of Tikal. The area covered is slightly over 1 square mile 1–5 Temples I–V; 6 Temple of Inscriptions; 7 Great Plaza; 8–14 Reservoirs; 8 Bejucal, 9 Causeway, 10 Temple, 11 Palace, 12 Hidden, 13 Madeira, 14 Perdido

why: this is an unplanned concentration of a basically dispersed population, with a slight increase in frequency and size of houses as one moves closer to the heart of the site itself, where the dwellings of aristocrats and bureaucrats alike would have been more splendid.

The same somewhat 'colloidal' appearance is typical of all other known Classic centres, which in the Central Area were always placed on hilltops or in other lofty positions so that they could be easily seen for several miles, if the trees around them were cut. They look, in fact, rather like artificial mountains. The same can be said for the sites of much of the Northern Area, although in the northern part of the Yucatán Peninsula, where ground water is scarce, the presence of large *cenotes* often determines the position of major ceremonial centres. But water was also scarce in the Petén, and at huge centres like Tikal there are several artificial reservoirs of some size, surrounded by embankments, which provided sufficient water to the inhabitants over the winter dry season.

Classic Sites in the Central Area

A Classic Maya centre typically consists of a series of stepped platforms topped by masonry superstructures, arranged around broad plazas or courtyards. In the really large sites like Tikal there may be a number of building complexes interconnected by causeways. Towering above all are the mighty temple pyramids built from limestone blocks over a rubble core. Although the temples themselves contain one or more corbelled and plaster-covered rooms, these are so narrow that they could only have been used on the occasion of ceremonies meant to be kept from plebeian eyes. Tall they are, but the Maya architects were not content and always added a further extension to the upper temple, a so-called roof comb (cf.

figure 25), which along with the temple façade was highly embellished with painted stucco reliefs.

The bulk of the construction at a Maya site, however, is taken up by the palaces, single-storied structures built on much the same principles as the temple pyramids but on much lower platforms and containing more plastered rooms (plate 38), sometimes up to several dozen in the same building. Occasionally, there may be one or two interior courtyards within the palaces. There is little agreement on just what a 'palace' was used for. Did the rulers live in these? They seem singularly uncomfortable (and bat-infested) to those archaeologists forced by circumstances to camp in them, and it seems more likely that the royal household was sheltered in perishable buildings which have not survived the lowland climate. It has also been suggested on the evidence of their cell-like rooms that they might have been monasteries or quarters for the priesthood, but it is entirely uncertain that there ever were ecclesiastical or monastic orders in Classic times.

In any Classic centre in the Central Area with a claim to importance, rows of standing stelae were placed in the stucco floors of the plazas, usually facing certain important temples but sometimes palaces as well. At times the stelae appear on platforms supporting temple pyramids, but the rule seems to have been that certain stelae were always associated with specific structures, for reasons until recently something of a mystery. Generally a stela will have a low, round, flat-topped 'altar' standing before it. The subject matter of the relief carvings on one or both stela faces seems always the same: a richly attired Maya (figure 22), generally a male, carrying peculiar emblems such as the so-called ceremonial bar or manikin sceptre, or else a similarly garbed person with spear and shield, trampling a captive underfoot. We shall examine these reliefs and the Long Count dates and glyphs which are inscribed on them in chapter 8, for the story that they tell is now becoming known.

Ball courts seem to be universal in the Central Area, but

Figure 22. Stela 4, Machaquilá, Guatemala (drawn by Ian Graham). Late Classic Period. The figure holds a 'Manikin Sceptre'

they are more frequent and better made in the south-east, at sites like Copán (plate 31). These courts are of stucco-faced masonry, and have sloping playing surfaces. Three stone markers were placed on each side, and three set into the floor of the court, but exactly what was the method of scoring in the game is obscure. Towards the western part of the Central Area, in centres along the Usumacinta river, sweat baths are known, possibly adopted from Mexico where such structures can still be found in many highland towns.

Awe-inspiring though the great Maya 'cities' are, there is little indication of any over-all planning in their arrangement. Rather, the typical centre seems to have grown by accretion as temples, palaces, and entire complexes were rebuilt over and over again through the centuries. There was a gradual accumulation of architectural features that seem to have had social and political functions of a special (but still undetermined) nature. Nothing could be more foreign to the Maya centre than the kind of grid plan seen in some of the great urban sites of Mexico, such as Teotihuacán.

Certainly one of the loveliest of all Classic Maya ruins is Copán (plate 30), situated above a tributary of the Río Motagua in a section of western Honduras famed for its tobacco. Stephens, who explored the site in 1839 (and bought it for fifty dollars!) called it 'a valley of romance and wonder, where . . . the genii who attended on King Solomon seem to have been the artists'. The principal temple pyramids rest on an artificial acropolis which has been partly carried away by the Copán River, but many of the structures remain intact. Among them is the Temple of the Hieroglyphic Stairway, completed in the eighth century A.D., with a staircase every one of whose sixty-three steps is embellished on the risers with an immensely long text of about 2,500 glyphs. The ball court at Copán (plate 31) is the most perfect known for the Classic Maya, with tenon sculptures in the shape of macaw heads as its markers. But it is the wonderfully baroque qualities of its carving in the round (plates 32, 33) which distinguish this site from all others, for the Copán artists worked in a greenish volcanic tuff superior to the limestone in use among

the Petén centres. Not only were doorways, jambs, and façades of the major temples ornamented with stone figures of
the Rain God, young Maize God, and other deities, but no
fewer than twenty stelae were carved and erected in Early
and Late Classic times, along with fourteen 'altars' (plate 34).
It appears that the majority of the stelae were placed on the
north end of the site, in a broad court bounded by narrow,
stepped platforms from which the populace could gaze upon
the spectacles involved with the stela cult.

Only thirty miles north of Copán lies Quiriguá, a far
humbler Classic centre which seems on the testimony of the
inscriptions to have been one of its suzerainties. Situated not
far from the western bank of the Río Motagua, in its lush
lower reaches, Quiriguá contains a few architectural groups
of no great distinction. Its enormous sandstone stelae (plate
36), however, are quite another matter; indeed Stela E, erected
late in the eighth century, might claim to be the greatest stone
monument of the New World, its shaft measuring 35 feet in
height. On the front face it is carved with the figure of a
bearded man holding a small hand shield and a 'manikin
sceptre' in either hand, while the sides are covered with texts
containing several Long Count dates. The great skill of the
Quiriguá sculptors can be seen in the grotesque full figures
which take the place of cycle glyphs in the inscriptions of
several other stelae, in the stone 'zoomorphs' representing
crouching earth monsters or sky deities with humans seated
among their snake-like coils, and in the richly embellished
boulders ('altars') (plate 35) associated with them.

It is more than likely that the ruins of Tikal (figure 21), in
the very heart of the Petén, were first encountered by the
brave Father Avendaño and his companions in 1695. Lost and
starving among the swampy *bajos* and thorny forests of
northern Guatemala, they came across a 'variety of old

buildings, excepting some in which I recognized apartments, and though they were very high and my strength was little, I climbed up them (though with trouble)'. Tikal, now partly restored by the University of Pennsylvania, is a giant among Classic Maya centres; it is the largest site in the Maya area, and one of the greatest in the New World. Particularly impressive are its six temple pyramids, veritable sky-scrapers among buildings of their class. From the level of the plaza floor to the top of its roof comb, Temple IV, the mightiest of all, measures 229 feet in height. The core of Tikal must be its great plaza, flanked on west and east by two of these temple pyramids, and on the north by the acropolis already mentioned in connection with its Late Formative and Early Classic tombs. Some of the major architectural groups are connected to the Great Plaza and with each other by broad causeways, over which many splendid processions must have passed in the days of Tikal's glory. The 'palaces' are also impressive, their plastered rooms often still retaining in their vaults the sapodilla-wood spanner beams which had only a decorative function.

Tikal is not particularly noteworthy for its stone sculptures. Among the many limestone stelae lined up in the Great Plaza before the acropolis, the best are of the Early Classic Period. None the less, there were great artists in the service of Tikal's rulers, for the fortunately preserved wooden lintels (plate 40) above the doorways of the temple pyramids are covered with lovely reliefs of Maya rulers in various poses accompanied by lengthy glyphic texts. Artistry of a different sort can be seen in the remarkable offerings accompanying the splendid tomb underneath Temple I, discovered in 1962 by Aubrey Trik of the University of Pennsylvania. In it a very great man had been laid to rest with his riches – his ornaments of jade and shell – and with food-filled pottery vessels. But what was really

Figure 23. Two incised bones from the Temple I tomb, Tikal. Left, three Cha

unusual was a large collection of bone tubes and strips (figures 23, 24) which had been delicately incised with scenes of gods and men carried out with the most extreme sophistication. The fine drawing and calligraphy gives us some idea of what a Classic Maya codex may have looked like, none of these bark-paper books having survived.

Figure 24. Incised bone of the Late Classic Period from tomb beneath Temple I, Tikal. A hand holding a brush pen appears from the jaws of a fantastic snake

There are ten reservoirs at Tikal from which the Maya obtained their drinking water, one of which was perforce refurbished by the modern archaeologists in lieu of any other potable source. These are often surrounded by artificial earthen levees, and contain sufficient water throughout the dry season. Some of them no doubt began as quarries, although the latter

ain Gods) are catching fish. Right, seven Maya deities travel in a canoe

are known in many other places around the site, where out-
crops and half-worked blocks of limestone still bear the marks
of the crudely chipped tools with which they were hewn by
the stone-masons of over one thousand years ago.

The many dozens of Classic Maya centres scattered over the
Petén, such as Uaxactún, Nakum, and Naranjo, are witnesses
to the importance of this region before its abandonment.
Maya sites are as numerous along the banks of the Usumacinta and its tributaries, in the south-western part of the Central
Area. Yaxchilán is a major centre strung out along a terrace
of the Usumacinta, with some of its components perched on
the hills above. While its temple pyramids reach no great
height, their upper façades and roof combs were beautifully
ornamented with figures in stucco and stone. Yaxchilán is
famous for its many stone lintels (figure 51), carved in relief
with scenes of conquest and ceremonial life (plate 39), with
which are associated dates and glyphic texts providing clues
to the real meaning of the Classic Maya inscriptions. All this
must wait, however, until chapter 8. Further downstream is
Piedras Negras (plate 44), which has also produced similar
data. This site is more extensive than Yaxchilán, and has a
large number of particularly fine stelae set in place before its
temples, as well as eight sweat baths, complete with stone-
built hearths lined with potsherds, masonry benches for the
bathers, and drains to carry off water used in the bath.

Few discoveries in the Maya area can rank with that of

Bonampak (plate 41), an otherwise insignificant Late Classic centre clearly under the cultural and political thumb of Yaxchilán. Bonampak, which lies not far from the Río Lacanhá, a tributary of the Usumacinta system, was first stumbled across in February 1946 by two American adventurers who were taken there by Lacandón Indians among whom they had been living. Three months later, the photographer Giles Healey was led by a group of Lacandón to the same ruins, and he was the first non-Maya to gaze at the stupendous paintings which covered the walls of three rooms in one of the structures.

The Bonampak murals (plates 42, 43), which can be dated to shortly after A.D. 800 on the basis of Long Count texts and stylistic considerations, obviously relate a single narrative, a story of a battle, its aftermath, and the victory celebrations. Against a background of stylized jungle foliage, a skirmish takes place among magnificently arrayed Maya warriors, while musicians blow long war trumpets of wood or bark. The scene shifts to a stepped platform in Bonampak itself (plate 43); the miserable prisoners have been stripped, and are having the nails torn from their fingers. An important captive sprawls on the steps, perhaps tortured to exhaustion, and a severed head lies nearby on a bed of leaves. A naked figure seated on the platform summit pleads for his life to the central figure, a great lord clad in jaguar-skin battle-jacket surrounded by his subordinates in gorgeous costume. Among the noble spectators is a lady in a white robe, holding a folding-screen fan in one hand. One of the final ceremonies includes a group of mummers fantastically disguised as water gods, accompanied by an orchestra of rattles, drums, turtle carapaces (struck with antlers), and long trumpets (plate 42). Perhaps the culminating scene is the great dance performed to the sound of trumpets by lords wearing towering head-dresses of quetzal plumes; in preparation for it white-robed Maya ladies seated on a throne draw blood from their tongues, and a strange, pot-bellied dwarf-like figure standing on a palanquin is carried on-stage. No verbal description could do justice to the beautiful colours and to the skill of the hand which executed these paintings. Suffice it to say that Bonampak has thrown an entirely new light on the warlike interests of the Maya leaders, upon social organization and stratification in a Maya centre, and upon the magnificence of Late Classic Maya culture in general, before time destroyed most of its creations.

The late Sylvanus Morley considered Palenque to be the most beautiful of all the Maya centres, albeit in comparison with a giant like Tikal it is of no great size. The setting is incomparable: Palenque lies at the foot of a chain of low hills covered with tall rain forest, just above the green flood plain of the Usumacinta. Parrots and macaws of brilliant plumage fly at tree-top level, and on rainy days the strange roar of howler monkeys can be heard near the ruins. A small stream runs through the site and is carried underneath the principal complex, the Palace (plate 49), by a corbel-vaulted aqueduct. A veritable labyrinth, the Palace is about 300 feet long and 240 feet wide, and consists of a series of vaulted galleries and rooms arranged about interior courtyards or patios, dominated by a unique four-storey square tower with an interior stairway. A Venus glyph painted on one of the landings suggests that the tower was used as an observatory, but it commands a wide view and could also have served as a watchtower. Arranged along the sides of two of the patios are grotesque reliefs, almost caricatures, of prisoners showing submission by the usual means, one hand raised to the opposite shoulder, and it could have been in these courts that the captured enemies of Palenque were arraigned. The Palenque artists excelled in stucco work (plate 45), and the exteriors of the pilasters ranged along the galleries of the Palace are marvellously embellished in that medium with Maya lords in relief, carrying the symbols of their authority, while lesser individuals sit cross-legged at their side.

Of the temple pyramids of Palenque, three were constructed in the mid seventh century A.D. on more or less the same plan, and must have served somewhat the same function. These are the Temples of the Sun, the Cross, and the Foliated Cross,

Figure 25. Cross section of the Temple of the Cross at Palenque, showing construction of the roof comb, vaults, and inner sanctuary

arranged about three sides of a plaza on the eastern side of the site. Each temple rests on a stepped platform (figure 25) with frontal stairway, each has a mansard roof with comb, and each has an outer and an inner vaulted room. Against the back wall of the latter is a 'sanctuary', a miniature version of the larger temple; in its rear is set up a magnificent low-relief tablet carved with long hieroglyphic texts and exhibiting the same motif, two Maya men, one taller than the other, facing each other on either side of a ceremonial object. In the case of the Temple of the Sun (plate 46), the most perfect of all Maya buildings, this central object is the mask of the Jaguar Sun, the sun in its night aspect, before two crossed spears. The two other temples have in its place a branching world-tree (which bears an astonishing resemblance to the Christian cross) surmounted by a quetzal bird. The exterior pilasters of the sanctuaries also bear stone reliefs of standing figures, the one on the right side of the Cross sanctuary unusual in that it shows an old man smoking a cigar.

From time to time over the past sixty years that excavations have been carried out at Palenque, finds have been made of fairly well-stocked tombs that were intruded into temple platforms and into the Palace itself. But these are nothing compared to the remarkable discovery made in June 1952 by the Mexican archaeologist Alberto Ruz. The Temple of the Inscriptions rests on a sixty-five-foot-high stepped pyramid approached by a noble frontal stairway. On the walls of its portico and central chamber are three panels containing a total of 620 hieroglyphs, with many dates the latest of which corresponds to A.D. 692. The floor of the temple itself is covered by large stone slabs, but Ruz was particularly curious about one which had a double row of holes provided with removable stone stoppers; on removing this it was clear that he had hit upon a vaulted stairway leading down into the interior of the pyramid, but intentionally choked with rubble. In four field seasons he had completely cleared the stairs, which changed direction half way down, finally reaching a chamber on about the same level as the base of the pyramid.

Figure 26. Stone tablet incised with the head of Chac, from the Late Classic Period at Palenque

It too had been filled, but on its floor were encountered the skeletons of five or six young adults, probably all sacrifices. At its far end, the passage was blocked by a huge triangular slab which filled the entire vault.

It was on removing this slab that Ruz first looked into the great Funerary Crypt (plate 51), a discovery rivalling that of Bonampak in importance. The chamber is thirty feet long and twenty-three feet high, and its floor lies underneath the frontal stairway but below the level of the plaza, some eighty feet down from the floor of the upper temple. Around its walls stride stucco relief figures of men in very archaic costume, perhaps the Nine Lords of the Night of Maya theology but it is equally possible that they were meant to be distant ancestors of the defunct. A huge rectangular stone slab, $12\frac{1}{2}$ feet long and covered with relief carvings, was found to rest on a monolithic sarcophagus within which a middle-aged man of unusual stature had been laid to rest. A treasure-trove of jade accompanied the corpse: a life-sized mosaic mask of jade (plate 47) was placed over the face, jade and mother-of-pearl disks served him as ear spools, several necklaces of tubular jade beads festooned the chest, and jade rings adorned his fingers. A large jade was held in each hand and another was placed in the mouth, a practice documented for the late Yucatec Maya, for the Aztec, and for the Chinese. Two jade figures, one representing the Sun God, lay at his side. Finally pottery vessels and two sensitively modelled heads in stucco were placed on the floor of the funerary chamber.

It is immediately evident that this great man, certainly a late seventh- or early eighth-century ruler of Palenque, had the Funerary Crypt built to contain his own remains; further, that he might have had the entire temple pyramid above it raised in his own lifetime. Thus it seems that the Temple of the Inscriptions was a funerary monument with exactly the same primary function as the Egyptian pyramids. And this, of course, leads one to look upon most Maya temple pyramids as sepulchral monuments, dedicated to the worship of deceased kings.

Classic Sites in the Northern Area: Río Bec, Chenes, and Cobá

The deserted forests of southern Campeche and Quintana Roo form the wildest part of the Maya region, but scattered through them are many ruined centres which have as yet been untouched by pick or spade. Our knowledge of these sites, as Miss Proskouriakoff has pointed out, is owed 'to the gum-chewing habit of our sedentary city-dwellers', for it is the chicle hunters who have come across them while searching for the sapodilla trees from which the gum is extracted. Several share in an aberrant architectural style named after the large site of Río Bec. Here showiness rather than function is what was apparently sought, for characteristic of this style of the Late Classic is the decoration of perfectly ordinary small 'palaces' with high towers imitating the fronts of temple pyramids; these towers are solid, however, the steps being impossibly narrow and steep, and the 'doorway' at the summit leading to nothing. It is as though the Río Bec architects wished to imitate the great Tikal temples without going to any trouble. In the Río Bec sites, such as Xpuhil and Hormiguero (plates 52, 53), we begin to see on façades and roof combs the elaborate ornamentation emphasizing masks of the sky serpent, which becomes of increasing concern to Maya architects as one moves further north into the Yucatán peninsula. To today's 'functionalists' the fakery of the Río Bec style is somewhat repellent, but no one could help but be awed at these mysterious sites crumbling in their jungle fastness.

Between the Río Bec area and the Puuc Hills of Yucatán is the Chenes, a well-populated zone of northern Campeche. Like those of Río Bec, with whom they must have been in close contact, the Chenes architects lavishly ornamented façades with sky-serpent masks and volutes, but the false towers of the former are missing. And, as at the Puuc sites to the north, the ornamentation consists of hundreds of small sculptural elements set into the buildings. One enters the front room through the fantastic jaws of the sky serpent, and is faced with tiers of such masks, one over the other, on the corners.

While the two sub-areas that we have been discussing are clearly intermediate in space and style between the Petén and the terminal Late Classic Puuc styles, there are centres in the wild eastern half of the peninsula which are obviously direct extensions of central Petén ideas and perhaps peoples. One of these is Cobá, a name implying something like 'ruffled waters', a fitting epithet since it was built among a small group of shallow, reedy lakes in northern Quintano Roo; the zone is frequented only by Maya hunters who occasionally burn incense before the stelae scattered among its ruins. Cobá is not a single site but a whole group linked to a central complex by long, perfectly straight masonry causeways usually called by the Maya term *sacbe* ('white road'). There are more than sixteen of these, but what the idea was behind their construction we cannot even guess, for quite often a *sacbe* several miles in length will reach a ruin of very paltry dimensions. *Sacbe* No. 1 is the strangest of all, for it continues west from Cobá in a generally straight direction for no less than 62 miles, finally reaching the site of Yaxuná, some 12 miles south-west of Chichen Itzá. Some have claimed that the Maya *sacbe* were arteries of commerce, but a purely ceremonial function is far more plausible.

The buildings of Cobá are in a sorry state of preservation, but there appear to have been temple pyramids and palaces like those of the Petén. It continued to be inhabited into Post-Classic times, for there are a few structures like those of Tulum (a very late town on the east coast of the peninsula), and there are references to Cobá in late Maya legends in which the centre is associated with the Sun God.

Classic Sites in the Northern Area: The Puuc

'If Yucatán were to gain a name and reputation', wrote
Bishop Landa in 1566, 'from the multitude, the grandeur and
the beauty of its buildings, as other regions of the Indies have
obtained these by gold, silver and riches, its glory would spread
like that of Peru and New Spain.' Landa was not exaggera-
ting, for ruins there are by the hundreds. Sylvanus Morley saw
this as evidence for what he called a 'New Empire' founded
by refugees from the derelict civilization of the Central Area,
his so-called 'Old Empire', and he claimed to find references
in the late Maya chronicles to a double-pronged migration
from the south. However, ceramics recovered from excavations, along with a better reading of the ethnohistoric sources,
led Eric Thompson and George Brainerd to the view that
many of the Yucatecan sites were coeval with the Petén centres
which were claimed to pre-date them.

It will be remembered that a group of very low hills, the
Puuc, is to be found in south-western Yucatán. It is there that
the dominant Classic architectural style of the peninsula takes
form, probably towards the close of the Late Classic Period.
The problem of dating is acute, for some of these centres are
mentioned in the chronicles by late upstart lineages who
claimed to have founded them, but there are truncated Long
Count dates painted on capstones in the late ninth and early
tenth baktun; the very latest reads 10.3.17.12.1, or A.D. 905,
but Thompson believes on excellent grounds that the Puuc
style may have lasted until 10.8.0.0.0 (A.D. 987), when the
Toltec invaders usher in the Post-Classic.

Characteristic of Puuc buildings are facings of very thin
squares of limestone veneer over the cement-and-rubble core;
boot-shaped vault stones; decorated cornices; round columns
in doorways; engaged or half-columns repeated in long rows;

and the exuberant use of stone mosaics on upper façades, emphasizing the usual sky-serpent faces with long, hook-shaped noses, as well as frets and lattice-like designs of criss-crossed elements. In the perfection of architectural technique, the Puuc is far ahead of the more sloppy Petén style.

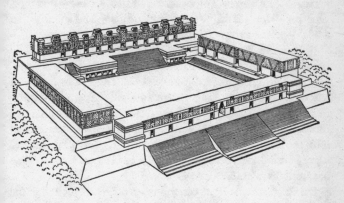

Figure 27. The Nunnery Quadrangle at Uxmal

Uxmal is by far the largest Puuc site, and one of the triumphs of Maya civilization. Traditionally, this was the seat of the Xiu family, but this was a johnny-come-lately lineage of Mexican origin which could not possibly have ever built the site. Uxmal is dominated by two mighty temple pyra-mids, that of the Great Pyramid and that of the Magician (the names come to us from the Spanish friars), the upper temple of the latter entered through a monster-mask doorway like those of the Chenes. Next to the Magician is the imaginatively named Nunnery (figure 27), actually a palace group made up of four separate rectangular buildings arranged around an interior court; although the group could be entered from the corners, the principal gateway with its corbel arch lies on the south side. The mosaic elements making up the masonry façades of the Nunnery Quadrangle are particularly interesting; they include miniature representations of the thatched-roof huts of the ordinary folk of the time. There are certainly hints in some of these elements of influences from Mexico, particularly from the Totonac site of Tajín in central Veracruz. One such element from the Temple of the Magician depicts a Tlaloc face surrounded by Mexican year-signs.

Below the Temple of the Dwarf, on its own artificial terrace, is the Governor's Palace, the finest structure at Uxmal and the culmination of the Puuc style. The upper façade or frieze of the three long interconnected structures of this building is covered by a fantastically elaborate mosaic of thousands upon thousands of separate masonry elements set into the rubble core, a symphony of step-and-fret, lattice-work, and sky-serpent-mask motifs combined into a single harmonious whole.

Other important Puuc ceremonial centres are situated in the hills to the south-east of Uxmal – Kabah with its rather hideous palace on which mosaic friezes of sky-serpent masks with hook-like 'noses' completely cover the façade; Sayil, having a particularly fine multistoried palace (plate 55) with central stairway (plus a number of curiously un-Maya phallic sculptures); and Labná, which is noted for its lovely free-standing arch (plate 54) and a temple pyramid and palace joined by a short causeway. In a narrow sense, Puuc architecture is confined to the Puuc hills, but from the description which we have from the pen of Bishop Landa, the colonial city of Mérida was founded upon the ruins of a Maya site called Tihoo, whose chief building was a palace seemingly exactly like the Nunnery Quadrangle at Uxmal. That the Puuc style reached east as well as north is evident at the great site of Chichen Itzá in eastern Yucatán, where a number of buildings at this otherwise Toltec centre closely resemble those to the west, with the proviso that Puuc veneer masonry is seldom present. Among these are the three-storey Nunnery (plate 50), the Akab Dzib ('dark writing', so called from the reliefs containing glyphic texts on one of the inner doorways), and the Temple of the Three Lintels; there may be more, but the problem of identification is aggravated by the syncretism between Maya and Toltec architecture during the subsequent Toltec occupation.

Art of the Late Classic

Late Classic Maya art evolves directly out of that of the early half of the period, but excepting the demonstrably late sculpture of the Puuc, there is very little outside influence still to be seen. Maya artists now were free to go their own way, evolving a remarkably sophisticated style as introspective as that of Asia and almost as 'naturalistic' as that of Europe and the Mediterranean. But the Maya were uninterested in three-dimensionality, although they could when they wished give depth to a scene by foreshortening. Their art is essentially a flat, painterly one, narrative and baroque, tremendously involved with ornament and grotesques but preserving what Proskouriakoff has called 'order in complexity'. Finally the Late Classic Maya were with their contemporaries, the Mochica of Peru, the only American Indians interested in rendering the uniqueness of individual characters through portraiture.

The Maya artists excelled in low-relief carving, and that is what most Maya sculpture is, whether on stelae, lintels, or panels. By the eighth century A.D., they had achieved a complete mastery of this medium, posing their figures in such a manner that in place of the rigid formality prevalent in earlier monuments, a kind of dynamic unbalance among the different parts of the composition was sought which leads the eye restlessly along. A lintel from Kuná (plate 56), a site only a few miles from Bonampak, provides a magnificent example of artistic contraposition, the goateed Maya resting on one leg and leaning forward clasping a ceremonial bar; but surely the perfection of relief carving was attained on the Late Classic tablets from Palenque (figure 26), particularly the Tablet of the Slaves which shows a great lord (plate 48) seated upon the backs of two barbaric-looking captives. Naturally, over such a wide area there were specializations, real schools of carvers at various sites. Copán, as has been mentioned, had a notable development of three-dimensional sculpture, while Palenque, on the other end of the Central Area, concentrated on reliefs carried out with extremely sophisticated use of carved and engraved lines.

Pottery objects of Late Classic manufacture run the gamut from crude, mould-made figurines and the ordinary pots and pans of everyday life to real works of art. Among the latter are the fantastic incense burners (plate 57) common at Palenque and in some of the Tabasco sites, consisting of tall, hollow tubes modelled with the figures or heads of gods and men, sometimes placed one on top of the other like Alaskan totem poles. Vertical flanges were placed on either side, and the whole painted in reds, ochres, blue, and white, after firing.

Jaina, a small limestone island just off the coast of Campeche and separated from the mainland by a tidal inlet, is one of the most enigmatic archaeological sites in the Maya area. For some reason known only to themselves, the ancients had used it as a necropolis, and it is close enough to the Puuc sites inland for it to have been their rulers who were buried there. Certainly the puniness of the temples constructed on the island is not in keeping with the great number of graves or with the magnificence of the offerings found in them. It is from these that archaeologists and looters have recovered the delicate, sophisticated figurines (plates 58–60) for which Jaina is famous. All objects are hollow and fitted with whistles at their backs; the faces were usually made in moulds, but these and other details were embellished by the fingers of the artist. The emphasis is upon portraiture of real persons, perhaps the occupants of the graves: haughty nobles and armed warriors, some with tattooed or scarified faces, beautiful young women and fat old matrons. Two common motifs are quite Freudian, a mature woman sheltering a grown man as though he were her own child (plate 58), and an ugly old man making advances to a handsome female. The only deity who appears with any frequency is the Fat God, who seems to have been popular among the Maya of Campeche.

Maya potters achieved chromatic effects of great brilliance in their vessels by firing them at low temperatures, sacrificing durability for aesthetic effect. Late Classic polychromes, generally deep bowls, cylindrical vessels, or footed dishes, are sometimes painted with the same narrative skill as the wall paintings exhibit. One such vessel is a ten-inch-high vase (plate 64) from an otherwise run-of-the-mill grave at Altar de Sacrificios in the Central Area. Justifiably described as 'a ceramic masterpiece', six strange figures, all of them dead or wearing the attributes of death and darkness, are painted on its exterior along with glyphs including a Calendar Round date corresponding to A.D. 754. The figure of an old man with closed eyes apparently dancing with a sinister, grossly fat snake is so well done that it suggests the employment of artists of genius in decorating pottery. Vessels could also be carved when leather-hard, just before firing, some excellent vases in this style from Yucatán depicting the Sun God seated among swirling volutes. Yucatán, though, had a greyish-brown pottery of its own called Slate ware (plate 61), sometimes plain but often carved with geometric ornaments, glyphs, or the figures of seated lords.

It is natural that the Maya lavished upon jade, the most precious substance known to them, their full artistry. That these jades were traded over considerable distances is evident from Late Classic Usumacinta-style pieces which were tossed into the Sacred Cenote at Chichen Itzá during the Post-Classic period, and some from the lowland Maya even found their way to Oaxaca and the Valley of Mexico. Most are very thin plaques with low-relief carving on one face, probably executed by tubular drills of cane used with jade sand, and by chisels of jade itself. A fine plaque from Nebaj in the Southern Area (plate 66) must be a product of a Central Area artist, and shows a recurrent theme, a richly dressed noble seated upon a throne, leaning forward to chat with a dwarf, perhaps a court buffoon.

Not only jade, but marble as well was worked by the lowland Maya lapidaries; but it must have been a rare substance, for objects made from it are infrequent. A fluted vase of translucent onyx marble (plate 62), with incising in Late Classic style, is a fine example of the genre. It is somewhat doubtful if the well-known marble vessels from the Ulua region of western Honduras are to be considered as Maya at all, but fragments from them have been found in deposits assigned to the ultimate phase of the Late Classic in British Honduras and Petén sites. That the Maya could impose their artistic conventions on any medium is apparent in the eccentric flint blades (plate 67) chipped to include human faces in profile, and small blades of obsidian (plate 65) incised with the gods of the Maya pantheon; these were favourite objects for placing in caches under stelae or beneath temple floors in Central

Area sites. Along the coast of Campeche, above all at Jaina (plate 68), art in carved shell reached a high level, the Maya typically painting the lily by inlaying these lovely objects with small pieces of apple-green jade.

The End of Classic Maya Civilization

Almost the only fact surely known about the downfall of the Classic Maya civilization is that it really happened. All the rest is pure conjecture. The sad story can clearly be read in the failure of centre after centre to put up commemorative stelae following the opening of Baktun 10 of Maya history, in the first half of the ninth century of our era. The katun ending date 10.3.0.0.0 (A.D. 889) was celebrated by inscriptions at only three sites. And the very last Long Count date to be recorded anywhere was the katun ending 10.4.0.0.0, incised on a jade from a site in southern Quintana Roo. Thus by the beginning of the tenth century the Classic Maya civilization had been extinguished in the Central Area, and we may be sure that most of its great centres were by then deserted, abandoned to the encroachments of the waiting forests. To the north, the Puuc sites may have been occupied until their overthrow by Toltec armies in the latter decades of the century.

Not only the demise of the Classic centres must be explained, but also the disappearance of the Maya people throughout most of the Central Area. Among the causes for these events which have been advanced are agricultural collapse, epidemic diseases like yellow fever, invasion by foreigners from Mexico, social revolution, forced evacuation by the early Toltec rulers of Yucatán, and even earthquakes and an unbalanced sex ratio! In desperation, some scholars have proposed varying combinations of all these factors, but it must be realized that there is little or no proof that any one of them prevailed. The agricultural-collapse theory, for instance, presupposes that the savannahs of the Petén resulted from over-exploitation of the land by Maya farmers, but we have seen that these grasslands were there before the people.

Nevertheless by the mid-ninth century there are indications of Mexican involvement with Maya sites, particularly those in the western part of the region. Seibal, for instance, erected a series of stelae early in Baktun 10 which show costume details and Tlaloc masks which look almost Toltec. It may be that the lowland Maya were already so weak from other causes that Mexicans could intrude without opposition into the Central Area. But until we can read the last inscriptions we shall never know what actually went on.

Whatever happened to the Central Area, we know that only a few groups stayed on, wandering through the now-empty centres and camping out like savages, or archaeologists, in the rooms of forgotten palaces – peoples like the Lacandón, burning copal incense before the strange depictions of mortal men and women who had now become gods.

[6] The Post-Classic

By the close of the tenth century the destiny of the once proud and independent Maya had fallen into the hands of grim militarists from the highlands of central Mexico, where a new order of men had replaced the intellectual rulers of Classic times. About the events that led to the conquest of Yucatán by these foreigners, and the subsequent replacement of their state by a resurgent but already decadent Maya culture, we know a good deal, for we have entered rather shakily into what might be called history. The traditional annals of the peoples of Yucatán, and also of the Guatemalan highlanders, which were transcribed into Spanish letters early in colonial times apparently reach back as far as the beginning of our Post-Classic era (figure 28) and are very important sources.

But they should be used with much caution, whether they come to us from Bishop Landa himself, from statements made by the native nobility, or from native lawsuits and land claims. These are often confused and often self-contradictory, above all since native lineages seem to have deliberately falsified their own history for political reasons. Our richest and most treacherous sources are the Katun Prophecies of Yucatán, contained in the so-called Books of Chilam Balam which derive their name from a Maya *savant* said to have predicted the arrival of the Spaniards from the east. The 'history' which they contain is based upon the Short Count, a cycle of 13 katuns (13 × 7,200 days or 256¼ years), each katun of which

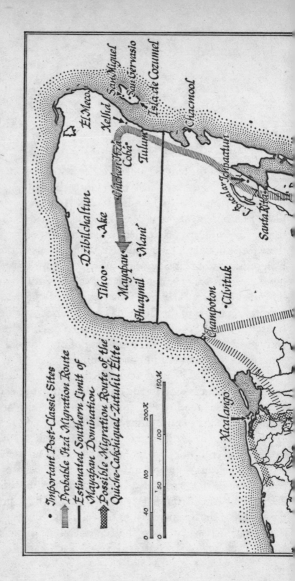

Important Post-Classic Sites

Probable Itzá Migration Route

Estimated Southern Limit of
Mayapán Domination

Possible Migration Route of the
Quiché-Cakchiquel-Zutuhil Élite

San Miguel
San Gervasio
Isla de Cozumel
El Meco
Xelha
Chichen Itza
Cobá
Tulum
Chicmool
Boca de Tepachtun
Santa Rita
Dzibilchaltun
Ake
Thoo
Mayapan
Uxmal
Mani
Huaynal
Champoton
Cilvituk
Xicalango

0   40   100   150   200 K
0   50   100   150 M

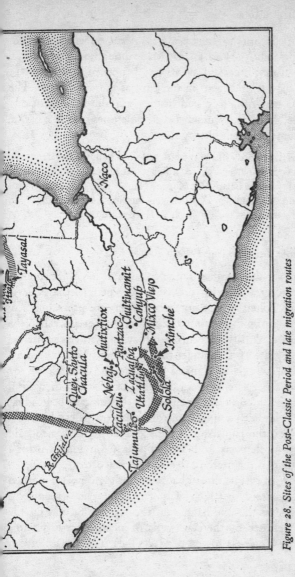

Figure 28. *Sites of the Post-Classic Period and late migration routes*

was named from the last day, always Ahau, on which it ended. Unfortunately, the Post-Classic Maya thought in purely cyclic terms, so that if certain events had happened in a Katun 13 Ahau, they would recur in the next of the same name. The result is that prophecy and history are almost inextricably entwined in these documents that sometimes read like divine revelation; one such history for example, begins:

This is the record of how the one and only god, the thirteen gods, the 8,000 gods descended, according to the words of the priests, prophets, Chilam Balam, Ah Xupan, Napuc Tun, the priest Nahau Pech, and Ah Kauil Ch'el. Then was interpreted the command to them, the measured words which were given to them.

The Toltec Invasion and Toltec Chichen Itzá

Into the vacuum created by the collapse of the older civilizations of central Mexico moved a new people, the Nahua-speaking Toltec, whose northern origins are proclaimed by their kinship with the non-agricultural barbarians called the Chichimec. Shortly after A.D. 900 they had settled themselves at the key site of Tula under the leadership of a king named Topíltzin, who also claimed the title of Quetzalcóatl or 'Feathered Serpent' (the culture hero of Mexican theology). Prominent among these people were the military orders that were to play such a significant role in later Mexican history – the Eagles, the Jaguars, and the Coyotes – and which paid homage to the war god Tezcatlipoca ('Smoking Mirror') rather than to the more peaceable Quetzalcóatl. According to a number of quasi-historical accounts of great poetic merit, a struggle ensued between Topíltzin Quetzalcóatl and his adherents on the one hand, and the warrior faction on the other. Defeated by the evil magic of his adversary Tezcatlipoca, the king was forced to leave Tula with his followers, most probably in A.D. 987. In one version well known to all the ancient Mexicans, he made his way to the Gulf Coast and from there set across on a raft of serpents for Tlapallan ('Red Land'), some day to return for the redemption of his people.

Wracked by further internal dissentions and deserted by most of its inhabitants, the Toltec capital was finally destroyed by violence in A.D. 1156 or 1168, but its memory was forever glorious in the minds of the Mexicans, and there was hardly a ruling dynasty in Mesoamerica in later days which did not claim descent from the Toltec of Tula. The city, which was certainly the administrative centre of an empire spanning central Mexico from the Atlantic to the Pacific, has been securely identified as an archaeological site in the state of Hidalgo, some fifty miles north-west of Mexico City, so that a good deal is known about Toltec art and architecture in its place of origin. Everywhere the Toltec went, they carried with them their own very unsympathetic style, in which there is an obsession with the image of the Toltec warrior, complete with pillbox-like head-dress with a down-flying bird in front, a stylized bird or butterfly on the chest, and carrying a feather-decorated *atlatl* in one hand and a bunch of darts in the other. Left arms were protected by quilted padding, and the back by a small shield. Prowling jaguars and coyotes, and eagles eating hearts dominate the reliefs which covered their principal temple pyramid, a testimony to the importance of the knightly orders among these militarists.

Now it so happens that the Maya historical sources speak of the arrival from the west of a man calling himself Kukulcan (*kukul*, 'feathered', and *can* 'serpent') in a Katun 4 Ahau which ended in A.D. 987, who wrested Yucatán from its rightful owners and established his capital at Chichen Itzá. Unfortunately, as the Maya scholar Ralph Roys has shown, the accounts of this great event are seriously confused with the history of a later people called the Itzá, who moved into the peninsula during the next Katun 4 Ahau, in the thirteenth century, and gave their name to the formerly Toltec site of Chichen. In any case, the Maya credited Kukulcan and his retinue with the introduction of idolatry, but the impressions left by him were generally good, for Bishop Landa states:

> They say he was favourably disposed, and had no wife or children, and that after his return he was regarded in Mexico as one of their gods and called Quetzalcóatl; and they also considered him a god in Yucatán on account of his being a just statesman.

The goodwill contained in these words is almost certainly due to most of the ruling houses of later times being of Mexican rather than Maya descent, for surely the archaeological record tells us that the conquest of Yucatán by the supposedly peaceful Topíltzin Quetzalcóatl and his Toltec armies

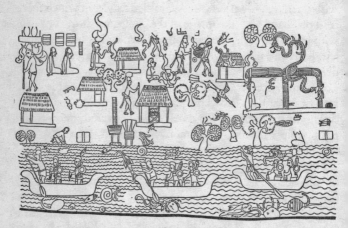

Figure 29. Wall painting from Temple of the Warriors, Chichen Itzá. Canoe-borne Toltec warriors reconnoitre the Maya coast

was violent and brutal in the extreme. The murals found in the Temple of the Warriors at Chichen Itzá, and the relief scenes on some golden disks fished up from the Sacred Cenote at the same site, tell the same story. The drama opens with the arrival of the Toltec forces by sea (figure 29), most likely along the Campeche shore, where they reconnoitre a coastal Maya town with whitewashed houses. In a marine engagement in which the Maya come out in rafts to meet the Toltec war canoes, the former suffer the first of their defeats. Then the scene moves to the land, where in a great pitched battle (commemorated in the frescoes of the Temple of the Tigers) fought within a major Maya settlement the natives are again beaten (figure 30). The final act ends with the heart sacrifice of the Maya leaders, while the Feathered Serpent himself hovers above to receive the bloody offering.

The Yucatán taken over by the Toltec exiles was then in its Puuc phase, but following the invasion, Uxmal and most other important Puuc centres must have been abandoned under duress. Chichen Itzá, which in those days seems to have been called Uucil-abnal ('Seven Bushes'), became under the rule of Topíltzin Quetzalcóatl the supreme metropolis of a united kingdom, a kind of splendid re-creation of the Tula which he had lost. New architectural techniques and motifs were imported from Toltec Mexico and synthesized with Puuc Maya forms. For instance, columns were now used in place of walls to divide rooms, giving an air of spaciousness to halls; a sloping batter was placed at the base of outside walls and platforms; colonnades of pure Tula type were built, which included low masonry banquettes covered with processions of tough Toltec warriors and undulating feathered serpents; and walls were decorated with murals in bands. And everywhere the old Maya masks of the long-nosed sky-serpent were incorporated in these new buildings.

Figure 30. Repoussé gold disk from the Sacred Cenote, Chichen Itzá. Two Toltec men-at-arms attack a pair of fleeing Maya. Diameter 8¾ in.

For not only was there a synthesis of styles at Chichen Itzá (figure 31), but also a hybridization of Toltec and Maya religion and society. Jaguar and Eagle knights rub elbows with men in traditional Maya costume and Mexican astral deities coexist with Maya gods. The old Maya order had been overthrown, but it is obvious that many of the native princes and priests were incorporated into the new power structure.

At the hub of Toltec Chichen stands its most important structure, the so-called 'Castillo', a great four-sided temple pyramid which Landa tells us was dedicated to the cult of Kukulcan. The corbel-vaulted temple at the summit of the four breathtaking stairways is a curious mixture of indigenous

Figure 31. Toltec warrior emerging from the jaws of a cloud-serpent, detail from a gold disk from the Sacred Cenote, Chichen Itzá

and foreign, sky-god masks embellishing the exterior, reliefs of tall war captains from Tula being carved upon the jambs of its doors. Inside the Castillo has been discovered an earlier Toltec-Maya pyramid, with beautifully preserved details, such as the chambers of the superstructure which contain a stone throne in the form of a snarling jaguar, painted red, with eyes and spots of jade and fangs of shell. Before it is one of the sculptures called 'chacmools', reclining figures with hands grasping plate-like receptacles held over the belly, perhaps for receiving the hearts of sacrificed victims. 'Chacmools' are ubiquitous at Tula and at Chichen, and are a purely Toltec invention.

From the Castillo may be seen the Temple of the Warriors (plate 71), a splendid building resting upon a stepped platform surrounded by colonnaded halls. It is closely planned after Pyramid 'B' at Tula, but its far greater size and the excellence of the workmanship lavished upon it suggest that the Toltec intruders were better off in Yucatán, where they could call upon the skills of Maya architects and craftsmen. The building is approached on the north-west through impressive files of square columns, which are decorated on all four faces with reliefs of Toltec officers. At the top of the stairs a 'chacmool' (plate 70) gazes stonily out upon the main plaza, while the entrance to the temple itself is flanked by a pair of feathered serpents, heads at the ground and tails in the air. Beyond them can be seen the principal sanctuary with its table or altar supported by little Atlantean Toltec warriors. All interior walls had been frescoed with lively scenes (figure 29) related to the Toltec conquest of Yucatán.

In 1926, just as restoration of the Temple of the Warriors by the Carnegie Institution staff was near completion, another such structure came to light underneath it, and from this, the Temple of the Chacmool, were recovered relief-carved columns still bearing the bright pigments with which they were painted. Two benches in the temple interior had been painted in a most interesting fashion, one with a row of Toltec leaders seated upon jaguar thrones identical to that in the interior of the Castillo, but the other with Maya nobles seated upon stools covered with jaguar skin, bearing manikin sceptres in Maya fashion. Could these have been quisling princes?

The splendid ball court of Toltec Chichen (plate 72) is the largest and finest in all Mesoamerica. Its two parallel, upright walls measure 272 feet long and 27 feet high, and are 199 feet

4

5

7

8

9

10

13

14

26

27

32

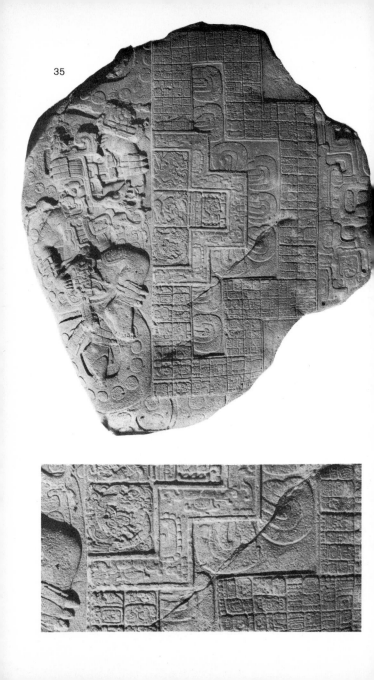

39

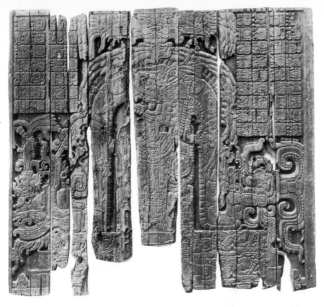

40

41

42

43

45

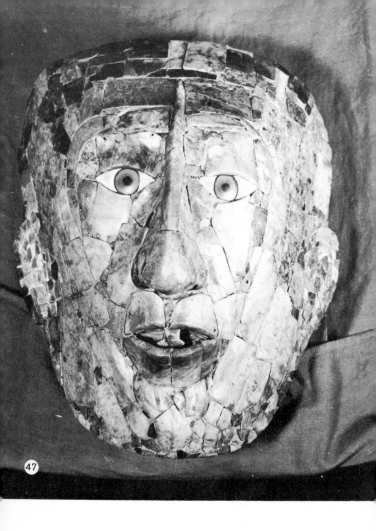

47

49

50

61

62

63

64

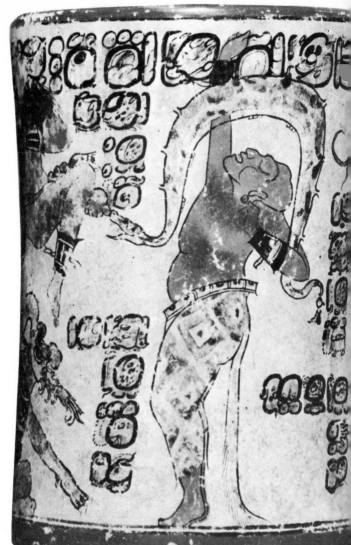

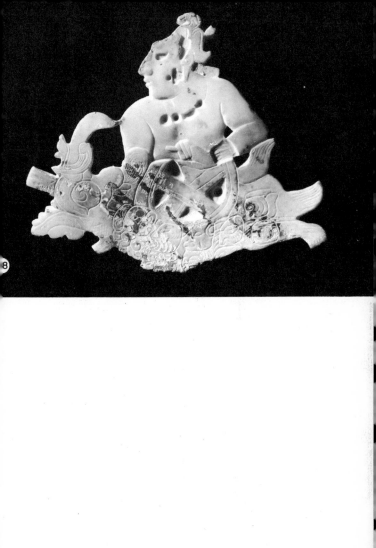

69

70

72

73

74

75

80, 81

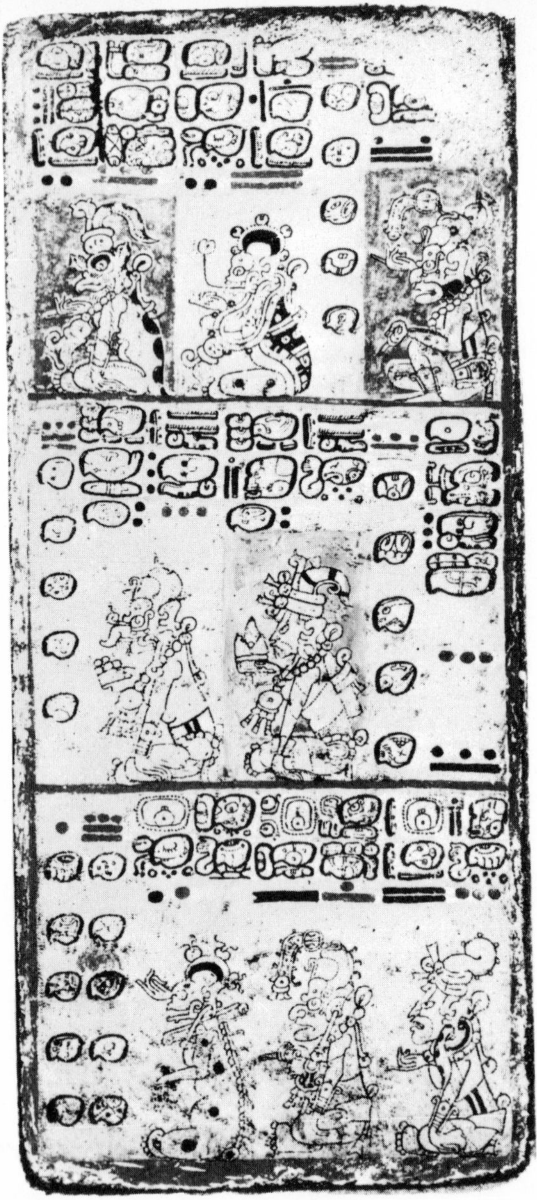

apart. At either end of the I-shaped playing field is a small temple, the one at the north containing extensive bas-reliefs of Toltec life. That the game was played Mexican-style is shown by the two stone rings set high on the sides of the walls, for a Spanish chronicler tells us that among the Aztec which-ever team managed to get the ball through one of these not only won the game and the wager but the clothing of the onlookers. Above the east wall of the court is placed the important Temple of the Tigers (plate 73), whose inner walls are beautifully frescoed with Toltec battle scenes, so detailed and convincing that the artist must have been a witness to the Toltec invasion.

Landa describes 'two small stages of hewn stone' at Chichen, 'with four staircases, paved on the top, where they say that farces were represented, and comedies for the pleasure of the public,' surely to be identified with the two Dance Platforms which have their facings covered with themes directly imported from Tula, such as eagles and jaguars eating hearts (plate 75). Human sacrifice on a large scale must have been another gift of the Toltec, for near the Ball Court is a long platform carved on all sides with human skulls skewered on stakes (figure 32). The name given to it, Tzompantli, is certainly apt, for in Post-Classic Mexico such platforms supported the great racks upon which the heads of victims were displayed. Each of the six Ball Court reliefs depicts the decapitation of a ball player, and it is entirely possible that the game was played 'for keeps', the losers ending up on the Tzompantli.

Finally the unlovely Caracol (plate 69) must be mentioned. This building which is actually in the Puuc section of Chichen, has been stigmatized by Eric Thompson as a 'two-decker wedding cake on the square carton in which it came'; it seems to date from very early Toltec times, but there are many

Puuc architectural features (such as sky-serpent masks) incorporated in it. Most probably it was an observatory, the snail-like spiral stairway in the interior giving access to exterior

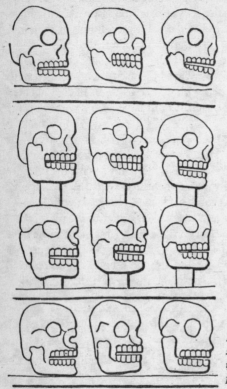

Figure 32. Bas relief of skulls skewered on a rack, from the Tzompantli, Chichen Itzá

openings from which sights could have been made on the sun and moon, as well as the cardinal directions, but it could also have been dedicated to the Kukulcan-Quetzalcóatl cult since circular temples were usually sacred to that god.

Chichen Itzá is most renowned not for its architecture, but for its Sacred Cenote, or Well of Sacrifice, reached by a 900-foot-long causeway leading north from the Great Plaza. From Landa's pen comes the following:

Into this well they have had, and then had, the custom of throwing men alive as a sacrifice to the gods, in times of drought, and they believed that they did not die though they never saw them again. They also threw into it a great many other things, like precious stones and things which they prized.

Shortly before the Spanish Conquest, one of our colonial sources tells us that the victims were 'Indian women belonging to each of those lords', but in the popular imagination the notion has taken hold that only lovely young virgins were tossed down to the Rain God lurking below its greenish-black waters. The late Dr Hooton, who examined a collection of some fifty skeletons fished up from the Sacred Cenote, commented that 'all of the individuals involved (or rather immersed) may have been virgins, but the osteological evidence does not permit a determination of this nice point'. A goodly number of the skulls turned out to be from adult males, and many from children, while pathology showed that 'three of the ladies who fell or were pushed into the Cenote had received, at some previous time, good bangs on various parts of the head ... and one female had suffered a fracture of the nose'!

As the great Mayanists Ralph Roys and A. M. Tozzer have stressed, the peak of the sacrificial cult at the Sacred Cenote was reached after the decline of Toltec Chichen, and continued into colonial times and even later. One crude rubber doll from the well has been recently shown to have wrappings of rayon cloth! None the less, many of the objects dredged from the muck at the bottom of the cenote are of Toltec manufacture,

including some marvellously fine jades and the gold disks
(figures 30, 31) already mentioned. For metals had now
appeared in the Maya area, although probably all casting and
most working was done elsewhere and imported, the many
copper bells and other objects from the well being of Mexican
workmanship. From places as far afield as Panama the local
lords brought in treasures of gold to hurl as offerings to their
Rain God.

This Toltec occupation has been detected at many other
places in the Yucatán Peninsula, and is everywhere marked by
the presence of the glazed pottery called Plumbate ware (plates
77, 78), produced in kilns along the Guatemala-Chiapas
border area near the Pacific shore. Plumbate vessels must have
been made to Toltec taste, for they often take the form of
Toltec warriors, but many are simple, pear-shaped vases
supported on hollow legs, very much like the carved painted
vessels (plate 76) also associated with the Toltec period in
Yucatán.

What finally happened to the Toltec? All indications are
that their mighty capital, Chichen Itzá, was abandoned in a
Katun 6 Ahau which ended in A.D. 1224, and they are heard
of no more. Another people now take the stage for a brief
moment and Maya culture lives a little while longer.

The Itzá and the City of Mayapán (A.D. 1224–1461)

The Toltec may finally have been accepted by the natives of
Yucatán, but the Itzá were always despised. Epithets such as
'foreigners', 'tricksters and rascals', 'the lewd ones', and
'people without fathers or mothers' are applied to them by the
Maya chronicles, and the phrase 'those who speak our language brokenly' shows that they could not have been Yucatec
in origin. Several scholars have suggested that at the beginning

of their history the Itzá were a group of Mexicanized Chontal-Maya living in Tabasco, where commercial connections with central Mexico were deep rooted. At any rate, while the Toltec lorded it over Yucatán, the Itzá were settled in a place called Chakunputun, probably Champoton on the coast of Campeche. About A.D. 1200 they were driven from this town (figure 28) and wandered east across the land, 'beneath the trees, beneath the bushes, beneath the vines, to their misfortune', migrating through the empty jungles to the region of Lake Petén Itzá, and to the eastern shores of British Honduras. Finally this wretched band of warriors found their way up the coast and across to Chichen Itzá, where they settled as squatters in the desolate city, in Katun 4 Ahau (A.D. 1224–44).

Leading the Itzá diaspora to northern Yucatán was a man who also claimed the title of Kukulcan, like his great Toltec predecessor of the tenth century, and he must have consciously imitated Toltec ideas, such as the cult of the Sacred Cenote, which now reached a peak of intensity. And yet another cult was initiated, that of the Goddess of Medicine, Ix Chel (figure 41j), with pilgrims from all over the Northern Area voyaging to her shrine on the island of Cozumel.

In Katun 13 Ahau (A.D. 1263–83) the Itzá founded Mayapán, some of the tribe remaining behind at Chichen Itzá, which now had lost its old name of Uucil-abnal and taken on its present one (meaning 'mouth of the well of the Itzá'). The wily Kukulcan II populated his city with provincial rulers and their families, thus ensuring a dominion over much of the peninsula. However, after his death (or departure), troubles increased, and it was not until about 1283 that Mayapán actually became the capital of Yucatán, after a revolt in which an Itzá lineage named Cocom had seized power, aided by Mexican mercenaries from Tabasco, the Canul ('guardians').

It may have been this sinister Praetorian Guard which introduced the bow-and-arrow to Yucatán.

Mayapán, which is situated in the west central portion of the peninsula, is a residential metropolis covering about $2\frac{1}{2}$ square miles and completely surrounded by a defensive wall testifying to the unrest of those days. There are over 2,000 dwellings within the wall, and it is estimated that between 11 and 12 thousand persons lived in the city. At the centre of Mayapán is the Temple of Kukulcan, a pitifully shoddy imitation of the Castillo at Chichen Itzá. The colonnaded masonry dwellings of important persons were near this, just as Landa tells us, but dwellings become poorer and poorer as one moves away from the centre. Each group of thatched-roof houses probably sheltered a family and is surrounded by a low property wall. The city 'pattern' is completely haphazard: there are no streets, no arrangement to be discerned at all, and it seems as if the basically dispersed Maya had been forced by the Itzá to live jam-packed together within the walls in a kind of urban anarchy. No real city had ever been seen before in the Maya area. On what did the population live? The answer is tribute, for Father Cogolludo tells us that luxury and subsistence goods streamed into the city from the vassals of the native princes whom the Cocom were holding hostage in their capital.

By this time, the Maya were thorough-going idolaters, and the excavators of Mayapán found a proliferation of shrines and family oratories, in which were placed brightly painted pottery incense burners of little artistic merit (plates 74, 82), representing Mexican gods like Quetzalcóatl, Xipe Totec (the God of Spring), and the Old Fire God, side by side with Maya deities like Chac the Rain God, the Maize God, and Itzamná.

In an ill-omened era Katun 8 Ahau (1441–61), fate began

to close in upon the Itzá. Hunac Ceel was then ruler of Mayapán, an unusual figure who achieved prominence by offering himself as a sacrifice to be flung into the Sacred Cenote at Chichen, and living to deliver the Rain God's prophecy given him there. The ruler of Chichen Itzá was a man named Chac Xib Chac. According to one story, by means of sorcery Hunac Ceel drove Chac Xib Chac to abduct the bride of the ruler of Izamal, whereupon the expected retribution took place and the Itzá were forced to leave Chichen. Next it was the turn of the Cocom, and a revolt broke out within the walls of Mayapán, stirred up by an upstart Mexican lineage named Xiu which had settled near the ruins of Uxmal. The Maya nobles of Mayapán joined the Xiu, and the Cocom game was up; they were put to death and the once great city was destroyed and abandoned for all time.

Those Itzá who were driven from Chichen Itzá were to be in evidence for several centuries more, however. Once again they found themselves as outcasts in the deserted forests, this time wandering back to the Lake Petén Itzá (figure 28) which they had seen in a previous Katun 8 Ahau. On an island in the midst of its waters they established a new capital, Tayasal, now covered by the city of Flores, chief town of northern Guatemala. Safe in the fastness of an almost impenetrable wilderness, their island stronghold was bypassed by history. Tayasal was first encountered by Hernán Cortés in 1524, while that intrepid conqueror was journeying across the Petén with his army to punish a rebellious insubordinate in Honduras, and he was kindly received by King Canek, whose name was borne by a long line of Itzá rulers. It was not until the seventeenth century that the Spaniards decided something must be done about this last, untamed Maya kingdom, and several missionaries were sent to convert Canek and his people – to no avail. It seems almost beyond belief that Tayasal fell to

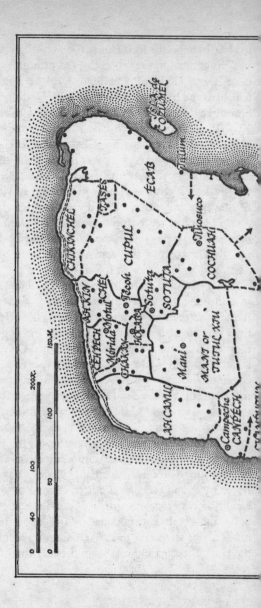

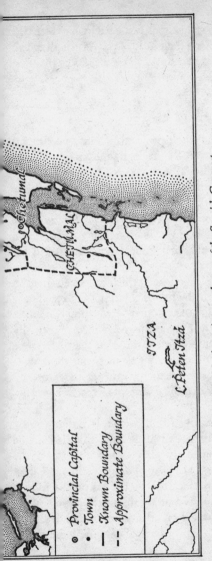

Figure 33. *The Independent States of the Northern Area on the eve of the Spanish Conquest*

the Spaniards only in 1697, and that while students at Harvard College had been scratching their heads over Cotton Mather's theology, Maya priests 2,000 miles away were still chanting rituals from hieroglyphic books.

The Independent States of Yucatán

With Mayapán gone, the whole peninsula fell into a condition of feudal anarchy. In place of a single, united kingdom were now sixteen rival statelets (figure 33), each jealous of the power and lands of the other, and only too eager to go to war in asserting its claims. Yet it is also true that the culture of the times, for whatever it was worth, was Maya, for much of what the Mexicans had brought was already forgotten and traditional Maya ways of doing things were substituted for imported habits.

There are few archaeological sites which can be assigned to this final phase, although the life of the times is exceedingly well described by Landa and other early post-Conquest writers who were able to question natives who had actually participated in that culture. We are sure that there were one or more major towns within each province, but these were chosen by the Spaniards for their settlements and most are buried under centuries of colonial and more recent constructions.

One site which was untouched, however, is Tulum (figure 34), a small town in the province of Ecab founded in the Mayapán period. Spectacularly placed on a cliff above the blue-green waters of the Caribbean, Tulum is surrounded by a defensive wall on three sides and by the sea on the fourth. Probably no more than five or six hundred persons lived there, in houses concentrated on artificial platforms arranged along a sort of 'street'. The principal temple, a miserable

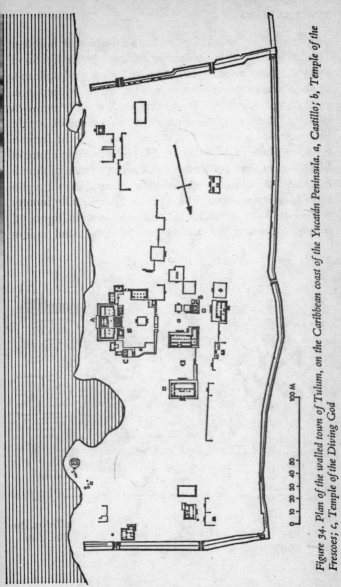

Figure 34. Plan of the walled town of Tulum, on the Caribbean coast of the Yucatán Peninsula. a, Castillo; b, Temple of the Frescoes; c, Temple of the Diving God

structure called the Castillo, and other important buildings are clustered together near the sea. On the upper façades of many of these dwarfish structures, which are of strikingly slipshod workmanship, are plaster figures of winged gods descending from above. Wall paintings have been found on both the interiors and outer surfaces of some temples, but the best preserved are in the two-storied Temple of the Frescoes (plate 79). Like the murals of the Late Post-Classic centre of Santa Rita in northern British Honduras, the style of these is less Maya than Mixtec, undoubtedly influenced by the pictorial manuscripts of that gifted people from the hilly country of Oaxaca. Yet the content of the Tulum frescoes (figure 35) is native Maya, with scenes of gods like Chac and various

Figure 35. Detail of wall painting in Temple of the Frescoes at Tulum. An aged goddess, probably Ix Chel, carries two images of the god Chac. Late Post-Classic Period

female divinities performing rites among bean-like vegetation. In one the Rain God sits astride a four-legged beast, for which there can be but one explanation: they had seen, or heard tell of, Spaniards riding on horseback. Not only Tayasal, then, but also Tulum must have lived for a while beyond the Conquest, protected by the dense forests of Quintana Roo.

Maya-Mexican Dynasties in the Southern Area

In the mountain valleys of highland Guatemala there were numerous independent nations on the eve of the Conquest, but the Quiché and Cakchiquel were the greatest of these. All indications are that they and their lesser neighbours, the Tzutuhil and Pokomam, had been there since very early times. And yet they claimed in their own histories that they had come from the west, from Mexico. As the Annals of the Cakchiquels relate: 'From the setting sun we came, from Tula, from beyond the sea; and it was at Tula that arriving we were brought forth, coming we were produced, by our mothers and fathers, as they say.'

As with the Yucatec in the north, the indigenous populations were ruled by dynasties of Mexican origin, and it is their legendary histories which we have. Leaving Tula perhaps among the hosts of the exiled Topíltzin Quetzalcóatl, they tarried near the Laguna de los Términos (figure 28), where they eventually seem to have clashed with the Itzá. Instead of heading north to Yucatán, they migrated south-east to Chiapas and Guatemala, where they quickly subdued the native peoples by the end of the eleventh century and became accepted as their natural leaders.

The *conquistadores* have described the splendour of their towns, such as Utatlán, the Quiché capital which was burned

to the ground by the terrible Pedro de Alvarado, or the Cakchiquel centre Iximché. These sites were placed in defensive
positions atop hills (plate 81) surrounded by deep ravines, and
are completely Mexican down to the last achitectural detail.
Typically, the principal building is a large double temple
with two frontal stairways, much like the Great Temple
of the Aztec in Tenochtitlán, and there usually is a well-
made ball court near by, for we know from the Popol
Vuh that the highlanders were fond of that game. Lastly
all buildings are covered in Mexican fashion with flat
beam-and-mortar roofs, the corbel principle being unknown
here.

Best preserved of these late highland centres is Mixco Viejo
(plate 80), capital of the brave Pokomam nation; the almost
impregnable site, surrounded by steep gorges, fell to Alvarado
and two companies of Spanish infantry only through treach-
ery.

The Spanish Conquest

'The raised wooden standard shall come!' cried the Maya
prophet Chilam Balam, 'Our lord comes, Itzá! Our elder
brother comes, oh men of Tantun! Receive your guests, the
bearded men, the men of the east, the bearers of the sign of
God, lord!'

The prediction came true in 1517, when Yucatán was discovered by Hernández de Córdoba, who died of wounds
inflicted by Maya warriors at Champoton. The year 1518 saw
the exploratory expedition of Grijalva, and that of the great
Hernán Cortés in 1519, but Yucatán was for a while spared as
the cupidity of the Spaniards drew them to the gold-rich
Mexico. The Spanish conquest of the northern Maya began
only in 1528 under Francisco de Montejo, on whom the

Crown bestowed the title of Adelantado. But this was no easy task, for unlike the mighty Aztec, there was no over-all native authority which could be toppled, bringing an empire with it. Nor did the Maya fight in the accepted fashion. Attacking the Spaniards at night, plotting ambushes and traps, they were jungle guerrillas in a familiar modern tradition. Accordingly, it was not until 1542 that the hated foreigners managed to establish a capital, Mérida; even so, revolt after revolt continued to plague the Spaniards throughout the sixteenth century.

The reduction of the Southern Area was largely the accomplishment of the resourceful but cruel Pedro de Alvarado, who arrived in Guatemala in 1523 fresh from his Mexican triumphs with cavalry, footsoldiers, and native auxiliaries. By 1541, the year of his death, the Quiché and Cakchiquel kingdoms had fallen under the Spanish yoke, and indigenous resistance was largely at an end.

But the Maya are, for all their apparent docility, the toughest Indians of Mesoamerica, and the struggle against European civilization never once halted. In 1847 and again in 1860 the Yucatec Maya rose against their white oppressors, coming very close the first time to taking the entire peninsula. As late as 1910 the independent chiefs of Quintana Roo were in rebellion against the dictatorial regime of Porfirio Díaz, and only in the last few decades have these remote Maya villagers begun to accept the rule of Mexico. Likewise the Tzeltal of highland Chiapas have repeatedly risen, most notably in 1712 and 1868. The Cholan-speaking regions west of Lake Izabal in Guatemala were feared by missionaries and soldiers alike as 'The Land of War', and the pacification of these Maya took centuries. The survival of the Itzá on their island Tayasal is a case in point; another is that of the wild and still independent Lacandón. No, the Maya were never completely conquered,

but their civilization and spirit were broken. As a poem from
one of the books of Chilam Balam puts it:

> Eat, eat, thou hast bread;
> Drink, drink, thou hast water;
> On that day, dust possesses the earth;
> On that day, a blight is on the face of the earth,
> On that day, a cloud rises,
> On that day, a mountain rises,
> On that day, a strong man seizes the land,
> On that day, things fall to ruin,
> On that day, the tender leaf is destroyed,
> On that day, the dying eyes are closed,
> On that day, three signs are on the tree,
> On that day, three generations hang there,
> On that day, the battle flag is raised,
> And they are scattered afar in the forests.

[7] Maya Life

While we have until this moment been dealing mainly with
the pots, jades, and ruins of a once great people, we actually
know a good deal more than this about the daily life of the
Maya, particularly of the natives of Yucatán on the eve of the
Conquest. For it is our good fortune that the early Spanish
missionaries were accomplished scholars, and that owing to
their eagerness to understand the nations they wished to
convert to the Cross they have left us with first-class anthropological accounts of native culture as it was just before they
came. So it is upon this foundation that we must interpret the
archaeological remains of the Post-Classic Maya – and the
Maya of the Classic as well.

The Farm and the Chase

Maya agriculture, which has been described in some detail in
chapter 1, was the foundation of their civilization. Maize,
beans, squashes, chili peppers, cotton, and various kinds of
fruit trees were cultivated. That the lowlanders have always
prepared their plots by the slash-and-burn method (plate 3) is
certain, but exactly how trees were felled prior to the adoption
of copper axes in the Post-Classic (and of steel ones in Colonial days) is unclear; perhaps they were merely ringed and
left to die. The times of planting were under the control of a
kind of farmer's almanac of which we apparently have

examples in the three codices. According to Landa, fields were communally owned and jointly worked by groups of twenty men, but this may not be very close to the real picture, as we shall see.

In Yucatán the Maya stored their crops in above-ground cribs of wood, but also in 'fine underground places' which might well be the *chultuns* so common in Classic sites. It is not certain that the lowland Maya ate *tortillas* (flat cakes), but other ways of preparing maize (figure 36) are mentioned in

Figure 36. Woman grinding maize on a metate, from a Late Classic figurine from Lubaantun, British Honduras

the early sources. These include *atole*, a corn-meal gruel which was taken with chili pepper as the first meal of the day; *posol*, a mixture of water and sour-dough carried in gourds to the fields for sustenance during the day; and the well-known *tamale*. The peasant cuisine (we know little of that current among the élite class) was largely confined to such simple foods and to stews compounded from meat and vegetables, to which were added squash seeds and peppers.

'Cash crops' were of prime importance to Yucatán. Cotton was widely grown, for the province was famed for its textiles which were exported over a very large area. Along river drainages in southern Campeche, Tabasco, and British Honduras and on the Pacific slope of Guatemala groves of cacao trees were planted, but in the north these were restricted to the bottoms of filled-in cenotes and other natural depressions. The chocolate bean from this tree provided the preferred drink of the Mesoamerican ruling classes, but well into Colonial times the beans served as a form of money in regional markets; so precious were they that the Maya traders encountered off the coast of Honduras by Columbus were said to have snatched up any that had dropped as though it was their own eyes that had fallen to the canoe bottom.

Every Maya household had its own kitchen garden in which vegetables and fruit trees were raised, and fruit groves were scattered near settlements as well. Papaya, avocado, custard apple, sapodilla, and the breadnut tree were all cultivated, but many kinds of wild fruits were also eaten, especially in times of famine.

There were several breeds of dogs current among the Maya, each with its own name. One such strain was barkless; males were castrated and fattened on corn, and either eaten or sacrificed. Another was used in the hunt. Both wild and domestic turkeys were known, but only the former used as sacrificial victims in ceremonies. As he still does today, the Maya farmer raised the native stingless bees, which are kept in small, hollow logs closed with mud plaster at either end and stacked up in A-frames, but wild honey was also much appreciated.

The larger mammals, such as deer and peccary, were hunted with the bow and arrow in drives (though in Classic times the *atlatl* and dart (figure 37) must have been the principal weapon), aided by packs of dogs. Birds like the wild turkey, partridge, wild pigeon, quail, and wild duck were taken with pellets shot from blow-guns. A variety of snares and deadfalls are shown in the Madrid Codex, especially a trap for armadillo.

In Yucatán fishing was generally of the offshore kind, by means of sweep and drag nets and hook and line, but fish were also shot with bow and arrow in lagoons. Inland, especially in the highland streams, stupefying drugs were pounded in the water, and the fish taken by hand once they had floated into

Figure 37. Huntsman slaying deer, on a figurine from Lubaantun, British Honduras. Late Classic

artificial dams; one of the beautifully incised bones (figure 23) from Late Classic Tikal shows that this was also the practice in the Petén. Along the coasts the catch was salted and dried or roasted over a fire for use in commerce.

Among wild products of the lowland forests of great cultural importance to the Maya was the resin of the copal tree, which (along with rubber and chewing gum!) was used as incense – so holy was this that one native source describes it as the 'odour of the centre of heaven'. Another tree produced a bark for flavouring *balche*, a 'strong and stinking' mead imbibed in vast amounts during festivals.

Industry and Commerce

Yucatán was the greatest producer of salt in Mesoamerica. The beds extended along the coast from Campeche, along the lagoons on the north side of the peninsula, and over to Isla Mujeres on the east. The salt, which Landa praised as the 'best ... which I have ever seen in my life', was collected at the end of the dry season by the coastal peoples who held a virtual monopoly over the industry, although at one time it was entirely in the hands of the overlord of Mayapán. A few localities inland also had salt wells, such as the Chixoy valley of Guatemala, but it was sea salt that was in most demand and this was carried widely all over the Maya area. Other valuable Yucatecan exports were honey, cotton mantles, and slaves, and one suspects that it was such industrial specialization which supported the economy, not maize agriculture.

Further regional products involved in native trade were cacao, which could only be raised in a few well-watered places, quetzal feathers from the Alta Verapaz, flint and chert from deposits in the Central Area, obsidian from the highlands north-east of Guatemala City, and coloured shells (particularly the thorny oyster) from both coasts. Jade and a host of lesser stones of green colour were also traded, most originating in the beds of the Motagua River, but some which appeared on the market could well have been looted from ancient graves.

The great majority of goods travelled by sea since roads were but poor trails and cargoes heavy. This kind of commerce was cornered by the Maya Chontal, such good seafarers that Thompson calls them 'the Phoenicians of Middle America'. Their route skirted the coast from the Aztec port of trade in Campeche, Xicalango, around the peninsula and down to Nito near Lake Izabal, where their great canoes put in to exchange goods with the inland Maya. However, a special group of traders travelled the perilous overland trails, guided by the North Star and under the protection of their own deity, Ek Chuah, the Black God. Markets are rarely mentioned where the lowland Maya are concerned, in contrast to Mexico where they were so large that the Spaniards were astonished, and it is probable that they were unimportant since there was little cause for heavy subsistence to change hands in this very uniform land. But we are told by one source that highland Guatemalan markets were 'great and celebrated and very rich', and these have persisted to this very day.

It was this trade that linked Mexico and the Maya, for they had much to exchange – especially cacao and the feathers of tropical birds for copper tools and ornaments – and it was probably the smooth business operations conducted by the Chontal that spared the Maya from the Aztec onslaught that had overwhelmed less cooperative peoples in Mesoamerica.

The Life Cycle

Immediately after birth, Yucatecan mothers washed their infants and then fastened them to a cradle, their little heads compressed between two boards in such a way that after two days a permanent fore-and-aft flattening (cf. plate 48) had taken place which the Maya considered a mark of beauty. As soon as possible, the anxious parents went to consult with a priest so as to learn the destiny of their offspring, and the name which he or she was to bear until baptism.

The Spanish fathers were quite astounded that the Maya had a baptismal rite, which took place at an auspicious time when there were a number of boys and girls between the ages of three and twelve in the settlement. The ceremony took place in the house of a town elder, in the presence of their parents who had observed various abstinences in honour of the occasion. The children and their fathers remained inside a cord held by four old and venerable men representing the Chacs or rain gods, while the priest performed various acts of purification and blessed the candidates with incense, tobacco, and holy water. From that time on the elder girls, at least, were marriageable.

In both highlands and lowlands boys and young men stayed apart from their families in special communal houses where they presumably learned the arts of war, and other things as well, for Landa says that prostitutes were frequent visitors. Other youthful diversions were gambling and the ball game. The double standard was present among the Maya, for girls were strictly brought up by their mothers and suffered grievous punishments for lapses of chastity. Marriage was arranged by go-betweens and, as among all peoples with exogamous clans or lineages, there were strict rules about those with whom alliances could or could not be made – particularly taboo was marriage with those of the same paternal name. Monogamy was the general custom, but important men who could afford it took more wives. Adultery was punished by death, as among the Mexicans.

Ideas of personal comeliness were quite different from ours, although the friars were much impressed with the beauty of the Maya women. Both sexes had their frontal teeth filed in various patterns, and we have many ancient Maya skulls in which the teeth have been inlaid with small plaques of jade. Until marriage, young men painted themselves black (and so did warriors at all times); tattooing and decorative scarification began after wedlock, both men and women being richly elaborated from the waist up by these means. Slightly crossed eyes were held in great esteem, and parents attempted to induce the condition by hanging small beads over the noses of their children.

Death was greatly dreaded by all, the more so since the deceased did not automatically go to any paradise. Ordinary folk were buried beneath the floors of their own houses, their mouths filled with food and a jade bead, accompanied by idols and the things which they had used while alive. Into the graves of priests they are said to have placed books. Great nobles, however, were cremated, a practice probably of Mexican origin, and funerary temples were placed above their urns; in earlier days, of course, inhumation in sepulchres beneath such mausoleums was the rule. To the Cocom dynasty of Mayapán was reserved the practice of mummifying the heads of their defunct lords, these being kept in the family oratories and fed at regular intervals.

Society and Politics

The ancient Maya realm was no theocracy or primitive democracy, but a class society with strong political power in the hands of an hereditary élite. To understand the basis of the state in sixteenth-century Yucatán, we have to go right to the bottom of the matter, to the people themselves.

In Yucatán every adult Maya had two names. The first came to him from his mother, but could only be transmitted from women to their offspring, that is, in the female line. The second derived from the father, and similarly was exclusively passed on in the male line. There is now abundant evidence that these two kinds of name represented two different kinds of cross-cutting and coexistent descent groups: the matri-lineage and the patrilineage. There were approximately 250 patrilineages in Yucatán at the time of the Conquest, and we know from Landa how important they were. For instance, they were strictly exogamous, all inheritance of property was patrilineal, and they were self-protection societies, all members of which had the obligation to help each other. Titles deriving from early colonial times show that they had their own lands as well, which is probably what Landa meant when he said that all fields were held 'in common'. As for the matrilineage, it probably acted principally within the marriage regulation system, in which matrimony with the father's sister's or mother's brother's daughter was encouraged, but certain other kinds forbidden.

While among many more primitive peoples such kin groups are theoretically equal, among the Maya this was not so, and both kinds of lineage were strictly ranked; to be able to trace one's genealogy in both lines to an ancient ancestry was an important matter. For there were strongly marked classes. At the top were the nobles (figure 38) (*almehen,*

Figure 38. Person of high rank in a palanquin, from a graffito incised on a wall at Tikal

meaning he whose descent is known on both sides), who had private lands and held the more important political offices, as well as filling the roles of high-ranking warriors, wealthy farmers and merchants, and clergy. The commoners were the free workers of the population, probably, like their Aztec cousins, holding in usufruct from their patrilineage a stretch of forest in which to make their milpas; but in all likelihood even these persons were graded into rich and poor. There is some indication of serfs, who worked the private lands of the nobles. And at the bottom were the slaves who were mostly plebeians taken in war, prisoners of higher rank being subjected to the knife (figure 39). Slavery was hereditary, but these menials could be redeemed by payments made by fellow members of one's patrilineage.

Figure 39. Standing captive, incised on a bone from the Temple I tomb, Tikal. Late Classic Period

By the time the Spaniards arrived, political power all over the Maya area was in the hands of ruling castes of Mexican origin. Yucatecan politics was controlled by such a group, which of course claimed to have come from Tula and Zuyuá, a legendary home in the west. In fact, any candidate for high office had to pass an occult catechism known as the 'Language of Zuyuá'. At the head of each little statelet in Yucatán was the *halach uinic* ('real man'), the territorial ruler who had inherited his post in the male line, although in an earlier epoch and among the highland Maya there were real kings (*ahau*) who held sway over wider areas. The *halach uinic* resided in a capital town and was supported by the products of his own lands, such as cacao groves worked by slaves, and by tribute.

The minor provincial towns were headed by the *batabs*, appointed by the *halach uinic* from a noble patrilineage related to his own. These ruled through local town councils made up of rich, old men, led by an important commoner chosen anew each year among the four quarters which made up the settlement. Besides his administrative and magisterial duties, the *batab* was a war leader, but his command was shared by a *nacom*, a highly tabooed individual who held office for three years.

The Maya were obsessed with war. The Annals of the Cakchiquels and the Popol Vuh speak of little but intertribal conflict among the highlanders, while the sixteen states of Yucatán were constantly battling with each other over boundaries and lineage honour. To this sanguinary record we must add the testimony of the Classic monuments and their inscriptions. From these and from the eye-witness descriptions of the *conquistadores* we can see how Maya warfare was waged. The *holcan* or 'braves' were the footsoldiers; they wore cuirasses of quilted cotton or of tapir hide and carried thrusting spears with flint points, darts with *atlatl*, and in late Post-Classic times, the bow and arrow. Hostilities typically began with an unannounced guerrilla raid into the enemy camp to take captives, but more formal battle opened with the dreadful din of drums, whistles, shell trumpets, and war cries. On either side of the war leaders and the idols carried into the combat under the care of the priests were the two flanks of infantry, from which rained darts, arrows, and stones flung from slings. Once the enemy had penetrated into home territory, however, irregular warfare was substituted, with ambuscades and all kinds of traps. Lesser captives ended up as slaves, but the nobles and war leaders had their hearts torn out on the sacrificial stone.

[8] Maya Thought

As in almost all the early civilizations of which we have record, it is extremely difficult to separate primitive scientific knowledge from its ritual context, but this should not lead one to suppose that a people like the Maya or the Sumerians had not evolved a considerable body of empirically derived information about the natural world. As we shall see, arithmetic and astronomy had reached a level comparable to that achieved by the ancient Babylonians and surpassing in some respects that of the Egyptians; but one should not exaggerate. Science in the modern sense was not present. In its place we find, as with the Mesopotamian civilizations, a combination of fairly accurate astronomical data with what can only be called numerology, developed by priests for religious purposes.

None the less our knowledge of ancient Maya thought must represent only a tiny fraction of the whole picture, for of the thousands of books in which the full extent of their learning and ritual was recorded, only three have survived to modern times (as though all that posterity knew of ourselves were to be based upon two prayer books and *Pilgrim's Progress*). These are written on long strips of bark paper, folded like screens and covered with gesso. According to the early sources, the Maya books contained histories, prophecies, songs, 'sciences', and genealogies, but our three examples are completely ritual, or ritual-astronomical, works compiled in the Northern Area during the Post-Classic. The Dresden Codex (plate 83) is the finest, and measures eight inches high and $11\frac{3}{4}$ feet long (figure 42); on internal evidence, some believe it to have been written in Campeche, but the Russian scholar Knorosov considers that it belongs to the Toltec-Maya period at Chichen Itzá. The Madrid and the very fragmentary Paris codices are much poorer in execution than the Dresden and somewhat later in date. Thompson has even suggested that a Spanish priest might have obtained the Madrid Codex at Tayasal.

To this must be added the Classic Maya inscriptions, or at least those parts which can be read or partially understood. And then we have a great deal of very valuable information on Maya ritual in the early post-Conquest accounts, and in various esoteric texts like the Books of Chilam Balam, written in Maya but transcribed into Spanish letters. From all of these documents it can readily be seen that Maya life was deeply imbued with religious feeling, and that ritual behaviour gave meaning and a sense of security to all strata of Maya society.

The Universe and the Gods

The idea of cyclical creations and destructions is a typical feature of Mesoamerican religions, as it is of Oriental. The Aztec, for instance, thought that the universe had passed through four such ages, and that we were now in the fifth, to be destroyed by earthquakes. The Maya thought along the same lines, in terms of eras of great length, like the Hindu *kalpas*. There is a suggestion that each of these measured thirteen baktuns, or something less than 5,200 years, and that Armageddon would overtake the degenerate peoples of the world and all creation on the final day of the thirteenth. Thus, following the Thompson correlation, our present universe would have been created in 3113 B.C., to be annihilated on 24 December, A.D. 2011, when the Great Cycle of the Long Count reaches completion.

Maya cosmology is by no means simple to reconstruct from our very uneven data, but apparently they conceived of the earth as flat and four-cornered, each angle at a cardinal point which had a colour value: red for east, white for north, black for west, and yellow for south, with green at the centre.

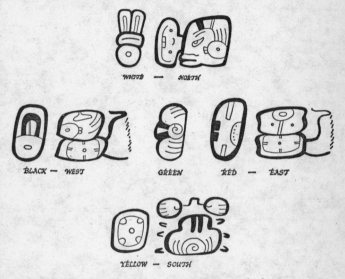

WHITE — NORTH

BLACK — WEST GREEN RED — EAST

YELLOW — SOUTH

Figure 40. Glyphs for the world directions and associated colours

The sky was multitiered, and supported at the corners by four Bacabs, Atlantean gods with the appropriate colour associations. Alternatively, the sky was held up by four trees of different colours and species, with the green ceiba or silk-cotton tree at the centre. Each of the thirteen layers of heaven had its own god, that of the uppermost being the *muan* bird, a kind of screech-owl. The underworld was nine-layered with nine corresponding 'Lords of the Night' ruling over it;

this cold, unhappy place was the final destination of most Maya after death, and through it passed the heavenly bodies such as the sun and moon after they had disappeared below the horizon.

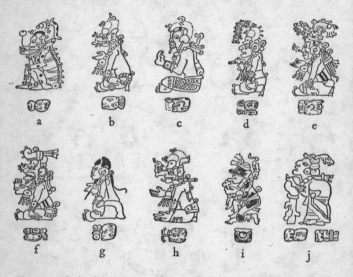

Figure 41. Gods of the Maya pantheon with their name glyphs, from the Dresden Codex. a, Death God; b, Chac, the Rain God; c, North Star God; d, Itzamná; e, Maize God; f, Sun God; g, Young Moon Goddess; h, Bolon Dzacab; i, Ek Chuah, the Merchant God; j, Ix Chel, Goddess of Medicine

Classic art and the Post-Classic codices suggest that the flat earth was thought of as the back of a monstrous crocodile resting in a pool filled with water-lilies. Its counterpart in the sky was a double-headed serpent, an idea probably stemming from the fact that the word for sky, *caan*, is a homonym of the word for snake. On the body of the sky-serpent are marked not only its own sign, crossed bands, but also those of the sun, moon, Venus, and other celestial bodies (figure 45).

Exceedingly little is known about the Maya pantheon (figure 41). That their Olympus was peopled with a bewildering number of gods can be seen in the eighteenth-century manuscript, 'Ritual of the Bacabs', in which 166 deities are mentioned by name, or in the pre-Conquest codices where more than thirty can be distinguished. This theogonic multiplicity results from the gods having many aspects. First, each was not only one but four individuals, separately assigned to the colour directions. Secondly, a number seem to have had a counterpart of the opposite sex as consort, a reflection of the Mesoamerican philosophy of dualism, the unity of opposite principles. And lastly, every astronomical god had an underworld avatar, as he died and passed beneath the earth to reappear once more in the heavens.

While some Maya sources speak of a one-and-only god (Hunab Ku) who was incorporeal and omnipotent, the supreme deity was surely Itzamná, 'Lizard House' (figure 41d), pictured as an aged man with Roman nose in the codices, the inventor of writing and patron of learning and the sciences. His wife was Ix Chel, 'Rainbow Lady' (figure 41j), the old goddess of weaving, medicine, and childbirth; it is possible that she was also the old Moon Goddess, but the snakes in her hair and the claws with which her feet and hands are tipped prove her the equivalent of Coatlicue, the Aztec mother of gods and men. All the other gods, including the Bacabs, were apparently the progeny of this pair.

The Sun God, Ah Kinchil (figure 41f), is very similar to Itzamná in the codices, and may have been one of his aspects. On his night journey beneath the earth he becomes the Jaguar God of fearsome aspect, often pictured on Classic monuments. It is believed that a young, half-naked lady prominent in the

Dresden Codex represents the Moon Goddess, Ix Ch'up, 'The Woman' (figure 41g), perhaps the consort of Ah Kinchil. Other celestial deities were the North Star (figure 41c), and various guises of Venus.

At the corners of the world were the benevolent Chacs, the Rain Gods (figure 41b), each of different colour but all deeply venerated by the Maya who saw them as manifested in thunder and lightning bolts (figures 23, 26). There were also four Pauahtuns, whose significance is unknown, and the quadruple Bacabs, each of whom presided over one quarter of the 260-day period in turn. Below, of course, were the hells presided over by a number of sinister gods, especially by Death himself (figure 41a), variously known as Cumhau, Ah Puch, and Cizin.

Further, there were patrons of the classes and professions. Heading this list is Kukulcan, god of the ruling caste; although his cult reached a peak in Toltec times, there are much earlier representations of feathered serpents at sites like Tikal. Several war gods were venerated by the soldiers, some of them clearly deified heroes, famed for their conquests. For the merchants and cacao growers there was Ek Chuah (figure 41i, plate 74), with black face and Pinocchio nose, but there were also patron deities of hunters, fishers, beekeepers, tattoo artists, comedians, singers and poets, dancers, lovers, and even suicides. Less easy to deal with are gods who may have been connected with the idea of lineage and descent; one of these is Bolon Dzacab, 'Many Matrilineages' (figure 41h), whose face with baroquely branching nose can be seen on the ceremonial bars and manikin sceptres brandished by persons of high rank on Classic monuments.

Priests and Rites

In contrast to that of the Aztec, the Maya clergy was not celibate. Sons succeeded their fathers to the office, although some were second sons of lords. Their title, Ah Kin ('He of the Sun') suggests a close connection with the calendar and astronomy, and the list of duties outlined by Landa makes it clear that Maya learning as well as ritual was in their hands. Among them were 'computation of the years, months, and days, the festivals and ceremonies, the administration of the sacraments, the fateful days and seasons, their methods of divination and their prophecies, events and the cures for diseases, and their antiquities and how to read and write with the letters and characters . . .', but they also kept the all-important genealogies. During the prosperity of Mayapán a hereditary Chief Priest resided in that city whose main function seems to have been the overseeing of an academy for the training of candidates for the priesthood, but in no source do we find his authority or that of the priests superseding civil power.

The priest was assisted in human sacrifices by four old men, called Chacs in honour of the Rain God, who held the arms and legs of the victim, while the breast was opened up by another individual who bore the title of Nacom (like the war leader). Another religious functionary was the Chilam, a kind of visionary shaman who received messages from the gods while in a state of trance, his prophecies being interpreted by the assembled priests. Every single Maya ritual act was dictated by the calendar, above all by the 260-day count. These sacred performances were imbued with symbolic meaning. For instance, the numbers four, nine, and thirteen and the colour directions appear repeatedly. Before and during rituals food taboos and sexual abstinence were rigidly observed, and self-mutilation was carried out by jabbing needles and sting-ray spines through ears, cheeks, lips, tongue, and the penis, the blood being spattered on paper or used to anoint the idols. On the eve of the Conquest such idols were censed with copal and rubber as well as ritually fed. Human sacrifice was perpetrated on prisoners, slaves, and above all on children (bastards or orphans bought for the occasion). Nevertheless, before the Toltec era animals rather than people may have been the more common victims, and we know that such creatures as wild turkeys, dogs, squirrels, quail, and iguanas were considered fit offerings for the Maya gods.

Our understanding of the Yucatecan ritual round is crippled by Landa's sporadic inability to distinguish between what he called 'movable feasts', i.e. rites determined by the 260-day count (figure 8), and those geared to the nineteen months of the 365-day Vague Year (figure 9). But apparently the greatest ceremonies had to do with the inauguration of the New Year (figure 42). These took place in every community within the Uayeb, the five unnamed and unlucky days at the close of the previous year, and involved the construction of a special road (perhaps like the Classic 'causeways') to idols placed at a certain cardinal point just outside the town limits; a new direction was chosen each year in a four-year counter-clockwise circuit. There were all sorts of omens, good or bad, for every year, but an inauspicious augury could be offset by expiatory rites, such as the well-known fire-walking cere-mony in which priests ran barefoot over a bed of red-hot coals.

Throughout the year there were agricultural rites and cere-monies for such important economic groups as hunters, bee-keepers, fishermen, and artisans, probably geared to the 260-day count if we may rely on the testimony of the Madrid

Codex, which seems mainly devoted to such matters. Increase of game, abundance of honey and wax, and so forth were the purpose of these activities, which so often take the form of the

Figure 42. New Year ceremonies in the Dresden Codex. Below, the Death God sacrifices before the New Year image; middle, the idol of Itzamná in the temple; above, the Opossum God carries out the image of the Maize God to a shrine at the entrance of the town

'sympathetic magic' defined by Sir James Frazer, for instance compelling the rain to fall by having the Chacs empty water from pots onto a fire.

Numbers and the Calendar

Otto Neugebauer, the historian of science, considers positional, or place-value, numeration as 'one of the most fertile inventions of humanity', comparable in a way with the invention of the alphabet. Instead of the clumsy, additive numbers used by the Roman and so many other cultures of the world, a few peoples have adopted 'a system whereby the position of a number symbol determines its value and consequently a limited number of symbols suffices to express numbers, however large, without the need for repetitions or creation of higher new symbols'.

The Maya, and probably the Olmec before them, operated with only three such symbols (figure 43): the dot for one, the bar for five, and a stylized shell for nought. Unlike our system adopted from the Hindus, which is decimal and increasing in value from right to left, the Maya was vigesimal and increased from bottom to top in vertical columns. Thus the first and lowest place has a value of one, the next above it the value of twenty, then 400, and so on. It is immediately apparent that 'twenty' would be written with a nought in the first place and a dot in the second, although it also had a symbol of its own. Professor Sánchez has demonstrated the ease with which calculations like addition and subtraction could be carried out in the system, but has also suggested in contradiction to others that multiplication and division, although not mentioned in the sources, would also have been possible.

And what kind of calculations were made, and for what purposes? Landa says that the purely vigesimal notation was used by merchants, especially those dealing in cacao, and he mentions that computations were performed 'on the ground or on a flat surface' by means of counters, presumably cacao beans, maize grains and the like. But the major use to which Maya arithmetic was put was calendrical, for which a modification was introduced: when days are counted, the values of the places are those of the Long Count, so that while the first

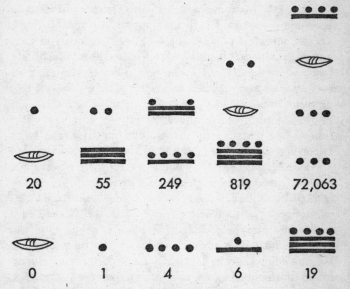

| 20 | 55 | 249 | 819 | 72,063 |

| 0 | 1 | 4 | 6 | 19 |

Figure 43. Examples of Maya vigesimal numeration

two places have values of one and twenty respectively, the third is to be thought of as a *tun* of 360 days (18 × 20), and so on up the line. For operating within their incredibly involved calendar, which among other things included the permutation of the Long Count with the fifty-two-year Calendar Round, the Maya priests found it necessary to construct tables of multiples; in the Dresden Codex, such tables include multiples of 13, 52, 65, 78, and 91 (the nearest whole number approximating one quarter of a year). Fractions find no place in their system – they were always trying to reach equations of cycles in which all numbers are integers, e.g. 73 × 260 days equals 52 × 365 days.

There are several kinds of dates (figure 44) expressed on the Classic Maya monuments and in the Dresden manuscript. Leading off a typical Classic inscription is the Initial Series, a Long Count date preceded by an Introductory Glyph with one of the nineteen month-gods infixed. This is immediately followed by the day reached in the 260-day count (figure 8), and, after an interval filled by several other glyphs, the day of the month (365-day count, figure 9). The intervening glyphs indicate which of the nine gods of the underworld is ruling over that day (in a cycle of nine days), and lunar calculations which will be considered later.

However, this is not the whole story, for there are usually a number of other dates on the same monument. These are reached by Distance Numbers, which tell one to count forwards or backwards by so many days from the base date, and, while the intervals are usually of modest length, in a few examples these span millions of years. And then there are Period Ending Dates in the inscriptions, which commemorate the completion of a katun, half-katun ('lahuntun', that is, ten tuns), quarter-katun ('hotun'), or tun. As an example one might cite the katun ending 9.18.0.0.0, which was celebrated all over the Central Area. 'Anniversaries' also dot the Classic inscriptions; these are Calendar Round dates falling at intervals of so many katuns or tuns from some date other than the above-mentioned Period Ending Dates.

Why this apparent obsession with dating and the calendar? What do all the dates on the Classic monuments mean? They have been until recently explained as the work of priests working out the positions of calendrical and celestial cycles in a

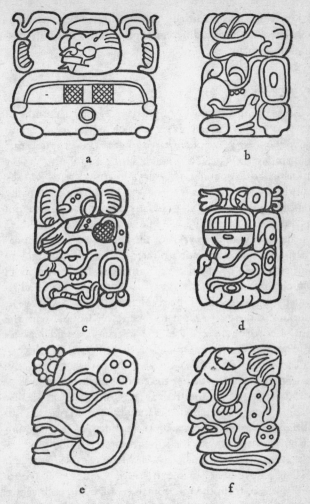

Figure 44. Glyphs for the cycles of the Long Count. a, Introducing Glyph; b, baktun; c, katun; d, tun; e, uinal; f, kin

religion which was essentially the worship of time itself. As we shall see, an utterly different explanation is not only possible, but probable.

The Sun and the Moon

To the Maya the round of 365 days – eighteen months of twenty days plus the five extra days of the Uayeb – was as close to the solar year as they cared to get. This 'Vague Year' began among the Yucatec of Landa's time on 16 July. Yet the earth actually takes about $365\frac{1}{4}$ days to complete its journey about the sun, so that the Vague Year must have continually advanced on the solar year, gradually putting the months out of phase with the seasons. We know that none of the Maya intercalated days on leap years or the like, as we do, and it has been shown that more sophisticated corrections thought to have been made by them are a figment of the imagination. Yet their lunar inscriptions show that they must have had an unusually accurate idea of the real length of the tropical year.

Curiously, the Maya went to far greater trouble with the erratic moon (figure 45d). In the inscriptions Initial Series dates are followed by the so-called Lunar Series, which contains up to eight glyphs dealing with the cycles of that body. One of these records whether the current lunar month was of 29 or 30 days, and another tells the age of the moon on that particular Long Count date. Naturally, the Maya, like all civilized peoples were faced with the problem of coordinating their lunar calendar with the solar, but there is slight indication that they used the nineteen-year Metonic cycle (on which the 'Golden Number' in the Book of Common Prayer is based). Instead, from the mid fourth century A.D. each centre made its own correction to correlate the two. However, in A.D. 682 the priests of Copán began calculating with the

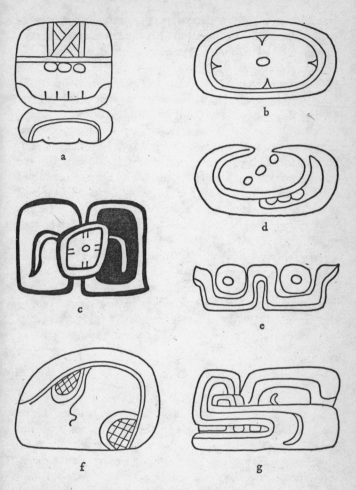

Figure 45. Glyphs for the earth and the heavenly bodies in the codices, a, Caan, the Sky; b, Kin, the Sun; c, solar eclipse; d, U, the Moon; e, Nohoch Ek, Venus; f, Cab, the Earth; g, believed to be Mars.

formula 149 moons = 4,400 days, a system which was eventually adopted by almost all the Maya centres. In our terms, they figured a lunation to average 29.53020 days, remarkably close to the actual value 29.53059.

Of great interest to Mayanists and astronomers alike have been the eclipse tables recorded on seven pages of the Dresden Codex. These cover a cycle of 405 lunations of 11,960 days, which conveniently enough equals forty-six times 260 days; a kind of formula with which the Maya were deeply concerned, for such equations enabled them to coordinate the movements of the heavenly bodies with their most sacred ritual period. The ancients had found out, at least by the mid eighth century A.D. but possibly much earlier, that lunar and solar eclipses (figure 45c) could only occur within plus or minus eighteen days of the node (when the moon's path crosses the apparent path of the sun); and this is what the tables are, a statement of when such events were likely. They also seem to have been aware of the recession of the node (or at least of its effect over long periods of time), and Eric Thompson suggests that the astronomer-priests accordingly constructed the tables anew every half-century or so.

The Celestial Wanderers and the Stars

Venus (figure 45e) is the only one of the planets for which we can be absolutely sure the Maya made calculations. Unlike the Greeks of the Homeric age, they knew that with the Evening and Morning Stars they were dealing with the same object. For the apparent, or synodical, Venus year they used the figure of 584 days (the actual value is 583·92, but they were close enough), divided into four periods of varying length – Venus as Morning Star, disappearance at superior conjunction, appearance as Evening Star, and disappearance at inferior conjunction. After five Venus 'years' its cycle met with the solar round, for $5 \times 584 = 8 \times 365 = 2{,}920$ days. Such an eight-year table can be found in the Dresden Codex.

Some have questioned whether the movements of planets other than Venus were observed by the Maya, but it is hard to believe that one of the Dresden tables, listing multiples of seventy-eight, can be anything other than a table for Mars, which has a synodic year of 780 days; or that the Maya intellectuals could have overlooked the fact that 117, the product of the magic numbers nine and thirteen, approximates the length of the Mercury 'year' (116 days). It has even been suggested that Jupiter was of interest to them. They were of course astrologers not astronomers, and all of these bodies which were seen to wander against the background of the stars must have influenced the destiny of prince and pauper among the Maya.

The Chaldean and Egyptian astrologers divided up the sky in various ways, each sector corresponding to a supposed figure of stars, so as to check the march of the sun as it retrogrades from sector to sector through the year, and to provide a star clock for the night hours. The zodiac of Mesopotamia is the best known of such systems. Did the Maya have anything like it? On this subject there is little agreement, but some have seen an indication of a partial zodiac on a damaged page of the Paris Codex, which shows a scorpion, turtle, and rattlesnake pendant from a celestial band. Very little is known of star lore among the Maya, but they did have constellations called *tzab* ('rattlesnake rattle', the Pleiades) and *ac* ('turtle', made up of stars in Gemini), with which they could tell the time of night; so a 'zodiac' is quite probable.

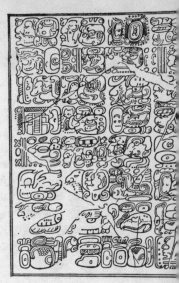

Figure 46. Tablet of the 96 Hieroglyphs, from Palenque. A very long text of the Late Classic Period, the content of which is mainly historical, though there are many calendrical glyphs

The Nature of Maya Writing

Few studies can have advanced so little with so much effort as the decipherment of the Maya script. This is not to say that a great deal cannot be understood, but there is a difference between unravelling a meaning for a sign, and matching it with a word in the Maya tongue. Progress has been most rapid on those glyphs which are of mainly calendrical or astronomical significance. For instance, by the mid nineteenth century the Abbé Brasseur de Bourbourg had discovered Landa's *Relación*, from which he was able to recognize day glyphs and interpret the bar-and-dot numeration in the codices. It was quickly discovered that Maya writing was to be read in double columns from left to right, and top to bottom. At the turn of the century all of the following had

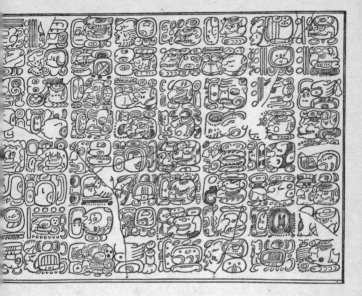

been correctly deciphered by scholars in Europe and America: the zero and twenty signs, the world directions and the colours, Venus, the months (also in Landa), and the Long Count. In a remarkable collaboration between astronomers and epigraphers, the mysteries of the Lunar Series had been unveiled by the early 1930s. But after these intellectual triumphs, fewer and fewer successes were scored, leading a few pessimists to the quite unfounded claim that there is little else in these texts but calendrical and astronomical mumbo-jumbo.

If we accept as a basic premise that there is some kind of system in the glyphs used in the non-calendrical texts (figure 46), then there is a limited number of possibilities as to what this might be. In a system of pictographs every sign is but a picture of the thing referred to; for some primitive peoples of the world, this suffices. However, one cannot draw a picture of everything which one might wish to communicate over long distances and through time. Accordingly, as Professor Lounsbury points out, every known script which is not merely pictographic has proceeded in two ways, that is, has moved in the semantic and the phonetic dimensions.

Moving semantically, to express a concept not easily visualized, one would picture something related to it, for instance a representation of a fire to express the word 'hot'; almost all of the world's scripts have adopted this principle at some time in their evolution. In its purest form such a system could be called ideographic, and could be 'read' without reference to any particular language. Numbers such as our own arabic ones are also ideographs for which all sorts of people have separate terms; so were the bars and dots of the Mesoamericans.

However, completely ideographic writing systems are virtually unknown, since most literate peoples have attempted to reduce the ambiguities which would be proliferated in them. Instead, there have been many developments along the phonetic dimension. Rebus or puzzle writing is the simplest form of this, in which an ideograph is now employed for its sound value, as the sign for 'fire' could be utilized in English as a sign meaning to 'fire' or sack a subordinate. As children we have all run across such examples of rebus writing as 'I saw Aunt Rose', all expressed in pictographs, and for peoples like the Mixtec and Aztec this was apparently the only script they knew.

However, there yet remain many uncertainties in even a rebus system. Most ancient scripts, like the Chinese, Sumerian, and Egyptian, are properly called 'logographic', in that each hieroglyph usually expresses a whole word which may be an ideograph or rebus sign, but which more often combines *both* semantic and phonetic components into a single compound sign. One of these compound types is a phonetic rebus to which a semantic determinant is added. The other is a semantic (that is, ideographic) sign linked to a phonetic complement. In time, as the language changes, the phonetic side of the script becomes less and less obvious, as with Chinese. But the real trouble with logographic systems is their sheer unwieldiness – to be literate in Chinese one must memorize at least 7,000 characters. The process of simplification necessarily concentrates on phoneticism, generally deriving something like a syllabary from the phonetic signs; since the phonemes, the smallest units of distinctive sound speech, are very much limited in any tongue, so are the number of signs in the syllabary. And finally, the alphabet arises as all the phonemes become separately distinguished, instead of appearing as syllables of the consonant-vowel sort. This is the ultimate step in the reduction of a writing system.

With these preliminary remarks, what kind of a system do we then find in the Maya script? Bishop Landa has given to us his famous 'alphabet' (figure 47) in which some twenty-nine signs are presented. Several extremely distinguished Maya scholars have stumbled badly in trying to read the codices and the inscriptions with Landa's treacherous 'ABC', while some have gone so far as to declare it a complete fraud. A more careful examination suggests that this is really not an alphabet in the usual sense. For instance, there are three signs for 'A', two for 'B', two for 'L'. Secondly, several signs are quite clearly glossed as syllables of the consonant-vowel sort, i.e. 'ma', 'ca', and 'cu'. We shall consider this important point later.

After the almost complete failure of decipherments along the strictly phonetic lines suggested by the Landa 'alphabet', a diametrically opposite line was taken by many authorities, namely that the script was purely ideographic, with perhaps a

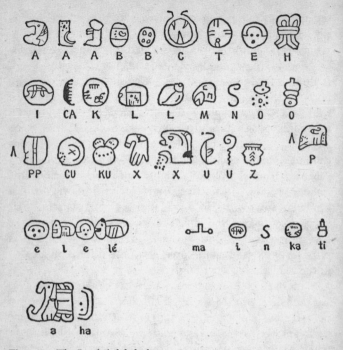

Figure 47. The Landa 'alphabet'

few rebus signs imbedded in the texts from time to time. That is to say, any one sign could have as many referents or associations as the priests could think up, and that only they could read the holy signs, which in general character were more ritualistic than linguistic. There is a striking resemblance between this position and that of the would-be decipherers of the Egyptian script before the great discoveries of Champollion.

This resemblance was not lost upon the Russian epigrapher

Yuri Knorosov, a student of Egyptian hieroglyphic writing. In 1952 he began publishing a series of studies which has re-opened the question of the Landa 'alphabet' and the possibility of phoneticism in the Maya script. About 287 signs, not including variants, appear in the codices. If the system were completely alphabetic, then the language of the texts would have contained this many phonemes; if purely syllabic, then there would have been half this number of phonemes. Both are linguistic impossibilities. On the other hand, if all signs were ideograms – representing units of meaning only – then the script represented an incredibly small number of ideas, certainly not enough for civilized communication. With this in mind, Knorosov has presented convincing evidence that the Maya were writing in a mixed, logographic system in which phonetic and semantic elements were combined as in Sumerian or Chinese, but that they also had a fairly complete syllabary.

Knorosov's starting point was Landa's 'ABC'. Eric Thompson had already demonstrated that the bishop's native inform-ant had mistaken his instructions: he gave the Maya sign not for the letter itself, but for the names of the letters; see, for instance, the first 'B', which shows a footprint on a road – 'road' is *be* in Yucatec, and this is exactly what the Spaniards call that letter. But the point is that this is really a partial and much flawed syllabary, not an alphabet, and Knorosov has been able to show that words of the very frequent consonant-vowel-consonant (CVC) sort were written with two syllabic signs standing for CV–CV, the final vowel (usually the same as the first) not being pronounced. The proof of phonetic-syllabic writing is, of course, in the reading, and a number of Knorosov's readings (figure 48) have been confirmed by the contexts in which the signs appear in the codices, especially by the pictures which accompany various passages of text.

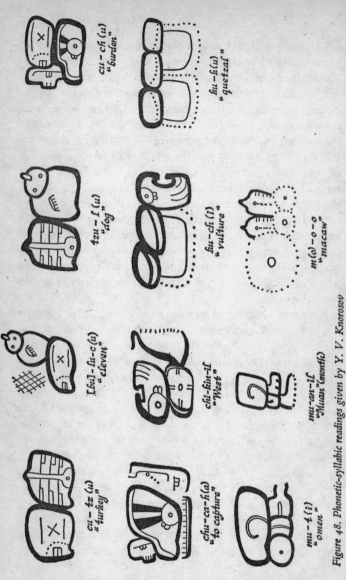

cu – ch (u)
"burden"

ku – k (u)
"quetzal"

tzu – l (u)
"dog"

ku – ch (i)
"vulture"

m(o) – o – o
"macaw"

[bul] – lu – c(u)
"eleven"

chi – kin – l
"West"

mu – an – l – (Chuen)
"Chuan (month)"

cu – tz (u)
"turkey"

chu – ca – h (a)
"to capture"

mu – t (i)
"omen"

Figure 48. Phonetic-syllabic readings given by Y. V. Knorosov

If this were all that needed to be done, it would be a simple job to read the Maya hieroglyphs, but the semantic dimension is very much there. There is a strong hint that phonetic complements were often attached to ideograms to help in their reading, either prefixed as a representation of the initial sound of the sign, or postfixed as the final consonant; these, if recognized, would notably advance the process of decipherment. There is indeed much to be done along many lines – it would take a lifetime, for instance, to fully verify all of Knorosov's proposed phonetic and semantic readings. We are a long way from cracking the Maya script, but it seems that the way has been shown.

It would be unfair to omit mention of other non-calendrical readings made by Eric Thompson and others. Thus Landa's *ti* is surely the locative prefix *ti* meaning 'at, on', and his first 'U' is the third-person possessive pronoun *u* ('his, hers, its'). Thompson has identified several signs for the numerical classifiers so prominent in the Maya language, such as *te* – an ideogram for *te*, 'tree, wood' – which is used in counts of time units.

The Content of Maya Writing

All three codices deal exclusively with religious and astronomical matters, as is quite obvious from the pictures of gods (plate 83) associated with the texts, from the tables, and from the high frequency of passages geared to the 260-day count. Thus we have in these texts little more than short phrases of esoteric significance, surely to be read in an archaic Yucatec, which often seem to match passages in the Books of Chilam Balam.

What, then, of the subject matter of the inscriptions? Until quite recently, the prevailing opinion was that this was in no way different from that of the books; and further, that all those dates recorded on the monuments were witnesses to some sort of cult in which the time periods themselves were deified. The great John Lloyd Stephens was of a different mind, writing about Copán: 'One thing I believe, that its history is graven on its monuments. No Champollion has yet brought to them the energies of his enquiring mind. Who shall read them?' The discovery within the last few years of the historical nature of the monumental inscriptions has been one of the most exciting chapters in the story of New World archaeology.

It began in 1958, when Heinrich Berlin published evidence that there was a special kind of sign, the so-called 'Emblem Glyph' (figure 49), associated with specific archaeological sites, and recognizable from the same kind of glyphic elements which appear affixed to each. Thus far the Emblem Glyphs for eight different Classic centres – Tikal, Piedras Negras, Copán, Quiriguá, Seibal, Naranjo, Palenque, and Yaxchilán – have been surely identified. Berlin suggested that these were either the names of the 'cities' themselves or of the dynasties which ruled over them, and proposed that on the stelae and other monuments of these sites their histories might be recorded.

The next breakthrough was by Tatiana Proskouriakoff of the Carnegie Institution, who analysed thirty-five dated monuments from Piedras Negras. The arrangement of stelae before structures she found was not random; rather, they fell into seven groups. Within a single such group the timespan covered by all the dates on the stelae is never longer than an average lifetime, which immediately raised the possibility that each group was the record of a single reign (plate 44). This has now proved to be so. The first monument in a series shows a figure, usually a young man, seated in a niche above a platform or plinth; on this stela two important dates are inscribed. One is

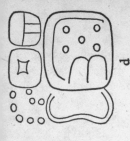
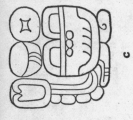

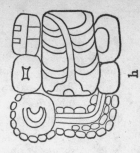

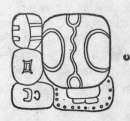

Figure 49. Emblem Glyphs from the Classic monuments. a, Tikal; b, Naranjo; c, Yaxchilán; d, Piedras Negras; e, Palenque; , Seibal; g, Copán; h, Quiriguá

associated with a glyph like an animal's head with a toothache (figure 50b), and has been shown to record the accession to power of the young man; the other appears with the 'up-ended frog' glyph (figure 50a) and is that same person's date of birth. Later monuments in a particular group celebrate what are probably marriages and the birth of offspring, and Proskouriakoff has been able to identify the signs for personal names and titles, particularly of women (figure 50e) who are quite prominent in Classic Maya sculpture. Military victories were also marked with great frequency, especially if an important enemy happened to have been taken captive by the ruler.

Thus the figures which appear in Classic reliefs are not gods and priests but dynastic autocrats and their spouses, children, and subordinates. As the records for one reign come to an end, the next begin with the usual accession motif. Perhaps the most complete documents we have for the temporal dynasties which ran the ancient Maya centres are carved on the many stone lintels of Yaxchilán (plate 39); from these Proskouriakoff has reconstructed the history of the extremely militant 'Jaguar' dynasty, which ruled the site in the eighth century A.D. The record begins with the exploits of a lord called 'Shield Jaguar'; he was succeeded in A.D. 752 by 'Bird Jaguar' (both these names recall the double names of the Yucatec – matronymic followed by patronymic), who was probably his son. As an example of how much of the writing that accompanies the reliefs celebrating the victories of this ruler can now be read or at least interpreted, we have Lintel 8 of Yaxchilán (figure 51), which begins with a Calendar Round date falling in A.D. 755. Below this is Knorosov's *chucah* or 'capture' glyph (figure 48), then a glyph resembling a jewelled skull, which is obviously the name of the prisoner on the right. Above right, the second glyph is that of the Bird Jaguar himself (the figure with

Figure 50. Historical glyphs in the monumental texts. a, Birthday Glyph; b, Accession Glyph; c, 'Shield Jaguar'; d, 'Bird Jaguar'; e, prefix for female names and titles

Figure 51. Lintel 8, Yaxchilán. A record of the capture of 'Jewelled Skull' and one other enemy by 'Bird Jaguar' and a companion

spear), beneath which is the Emblem Glyph of Yaxchilán (figure 49).

Of special interest are those inscriptions which indicate the interference of some centres with the destinies of others. For instance, the Yaxchilán Emblem Glyph appears with one of the most prominent women in the Bonampak frescoes (plate 43), and the glyph for Tikal quite frequently on monuments at Naranjo. Piedras Negras is not far downstream from Yaxchilán, and the famous Lintel 3 from that site is now believed to show a Yaxchilán ruler presiding over a council called in the late eighth century to choose a successor to the Piedras Negras throne.

Then why the Lunar Series and the calculations far into the past and future? Because the Classic Maya élite believed in astrology, and must have consulted their priests for lunar and other cosmic auguries at every important civil event, as did the Babylonians, Etruscans, Egyptians, and many other peoples of the Old World. There is a logic to astrology which not only the ancients have found compelling – Kepler and Newton did likewise – so we need not condemn the Maya for their beliefs. Another Maya concern was with lineage, and we find figures and dates on some monuments which can only refer to distant ancestors. Thus Berlin has been able to show that the dates in inscriptions of the Temple of the Cross at Palenque (figure 25) fall into three groups. The first are so ancient that they could only be referring back to deified ancestors of a legendary epoch; the next may have to do with distant progenitors of a more intermediate time; and the third are connected with contemporary historical events.

So far no Champollion has appeared who could read the Maya inscriptions *in toto*. But it should be remembered that it was the identification of personal names and titles in the Egyptian script that enabled that great scholar to do what he did. Indeed the recognition of the real subject matter of the Maya monumental texts has opened the way to their eventual decipherment.

Select Bibliography

For a really complete listing of works on Maya archaeology, the reader is referred to 'Bibliografía de Arqueología y Etnografía: Mesoamérica y Norte de México, 1514–1960' by Ignacio Bernal (*Instituto Nacional de Antropología e Historia, Memorias*, VII, Mexico, 1962), which contains over 3,800 titles on the subject. I have tried to concentrate on those articles and volumes which I have found most useful in the preparation of this book, and which might be of interest to those wishing to follow certain topics further.

CHAPTER 1

General works on Mesoamerica and the Maya

BLOM, FRANS, and OLIVER LA FARGE. *Tribes and Temples.* 2 vols., New Orleans, 1926.

BRAINERD, GEORGE W. *The Maya Civilization.* Los Angeles, 1954.

COVARRUBIAS, MIGUEL. *Indian Art of Mexico and Central America.* New York, 1957.

GIRARD, RAFAEL. *Los Mayas Eternos.* Mexico, 1962.

HOLMES, WILLIAM H. *Archaeological Studies among the Ancient Cities of Mexico,* 2 vols. Chicago, 1895–7.

KIDDER II, ALFRED, and CARLOS SAMAYOA CHINCHILLA. *The Art of the Ancient Maya.* New York, 1959.

KIRCHHOFF, PAUL. 'Meso-America', in *Heritage of Conquest*, Sol Tax (ed.), 17–30. Glencoe, Illinois, 1952.

MARQUINA, IGNACIO. *Arquitectura Prehispánica.* Mexico, 1951.

MAUDSLAY, ALFRED P. *Biologia Centrali-Americana, Archaeology.* Text and 4 vols. of plates. London, 1889–1902.

MORLEY, SYLVANUS G. *The Ancient Maya*, 3rd edition, revised by George W. Brainerd. Stanford, 1956.

PROSKOURIAKOFF, TATIANA. 'An album of Maya architecture', *Carnegie Institution of Washington*, Publ. 558. Washington, 1946.

SPINDEN, HERBERT J. 'A study of Maya art', *Memoirs of the Peabody Museum of Archaeology and Ethnology, Harvard University*, vol. 6. Cambridge, 1913.

STEPHENS, JOHN L. *Incidents of Travel in Central America, Chiapas, and Yucatan*, 2 vols. New York, 1841.

—, *Incidents of Travel in Yucatan*. 2 vols. New York, 1843.

STIERLIN, HENRI. *Maya: Guatemala, Honduras et Yucatan*. Fribourg, 1964.

THE MAYA AND THEIR NEIGHBORS. Dedicated to Alfred M. Tozzer. New York, 1941.

THOMPSON, J. ERIC S. 'A trial survey of the southern Maya area', *American Antiquity*, vol. 9, no. 1, 106–34. Menasha, 1943.

—, 'A trial survey of the northern Maya area', *American Antiquity*, vol. 11, no. 1, 2–4, Menasha, 1945.

—, *The Rise and Fall of Maya Civilization*. Norman, 1954.

TOZZER, ALFRED M. (ed.). 'Landa's Relación de las Cosas de Yucatán', *Papers of the Peabody Museum of Archaeology and Ethnology, Harvard University*, vol. 18. Cambridge, 1941. (Thanks to the extensive notes which accompany Landa's text, this is virtually an encyclopedia of ancient Maya life.)

VOGT, EVON Z., and ALBERTO RUZ. *Desarrollo Cultural de los Mayas*. Mexico, 1964. (A very up-to-date collection of essays by various authors.)

The setting

BRAINERD, GEORGE W. 'Changing living patterns of the Yucatan Maya', *American Antiquity*, vol. 22, no. 2, 162–4. Salt Lake City, 1956.

COWGILL, URSULA M. 'An agricultural study of the southern Maya lowlands', *American Anthropologist*, vol. 64, no. 2, 273–86. Menasha, 1962.

MCBRYDE, FELIX W. 'Cultural and historical geography of south-west Guatemala', *Smithsonian Institution of Social Anthropology*, Publ. no. 4. Washington, 1945.

WRIGHT, A. C. S., *et al. Land in British Honduras*. London, 1959.

Maya linguistic distributions

MCQUOWN, NORMAN A. 'The classification of the Maya languages', *International Journal of American Linguistics*, vol. 22, 191–5. 1956.

—, 'Los orígenes y la diferenciación de los mayas según se infiere del estudio comparativo de las lenguas mayanas', in *Desarrollo Cultural de los Mayas*, 49–80. Mexico, 1964.

SWADESH, MAURICE. 'Interrelaciones de las lenguas mayenses', *Anales del Instituto Nacional de Antropología e Historia*, XIII, 231–67. Mexico,1961.

CHAPTER 2

BRAINERD, GEORGE W. 'The archaeological ceramics of Yucatan', *Anthropological Records*, 19. Berkeley and Los Angeles, 1958.

COE, MICHAEL D. 'A fluted point from highland Guatemala', *American Antiquity*, vol. 25, no. 3, 412–3. Salt Lake City, 1960.

—, 'La Victoria, an early site on the Pacific coast of Guatemala', *Papers of the Peabody Museum of Archaeology and Ethnology, Harvard University*, vol. 53. Cambridge, 1961.

COE, MICHAEL D., and KENT V. FLANNERY. 'The pre-Columbian obsidian industry of El Chayal, Guatemala', *American Antiquity*, vol. 30, no. 1, 43–9. Salt Lake City, 1964.

MACNEISH, RICHARD S. 'The origins of New World civilization', *Scientific American*, vol. 211, no. 5, 29–37. New York, 1964.

MACNEISH, RICHARD S., and FREDERICK A. PETERSON. 'The Santa Marta Rock Shelter, Ocozocoautla, Chiapas, Mexico', *Papers of the New World Archaeological Foundation*, No. 14. Provo, 1962.

SHOOK, EDWIN M. 'The present status of research on the Pre-Classic horizons in Guatemala', in *The Civilizations of Ancient America*, Sol Tax (ed.), 93–100. Chicago, 1951.

SMITH, ROBERT E. 'Ceramic sequence at Uaxactun, Guatemala', *Middle American Research Institute*, Publ. 20. 2 vols. New Orleans, 1955.

WAUCHOPE, ROBERT. 'Implications of radiocarbon dates from Middle and South America', *Middle American Research Reports*, vol. 2, no. 2. New Orleans, 1954.

CHAPTER 3

BRAINERD, GEORGE W. 'Early ceramic horizons in Yucatan', in *The Civilizations of Ancient America*, Sol Tax, (ed.), 72–8. Chicago, 1951.

COE, MICHAEL D. 'Cycle 7 monuments in Middle America: a reconsideration', *American Anthropologist*, vol. 59, no. 4, 597–611. Menasha, 1957.

COE, WILLIAM R. 'Tikal, Guatemala, and emergent Maya civilization', *Science*, vol. 147, no. 3664, 1401–91. Washington, 1965.

MORLEY, SYLVANUS G. and FRANCES R. 'The age and provenance of the Leyden Plate', *Carnegie Institution of Washington, Contributions to American Anthropology and History*, no. 24. Washington, 1939.

PARSONS, LEE A. 'Boulder sculpture on the Pacific coast of Guatemala', *Archaeology*, vol. 18, no. 2, 132–44. Brattleboro, Vermont, 1965.

RICKETSON, OLIVER G. and EDITH B. 'Uaxactun, Guatemala, Group E— 1926–1931', *Carnegie Institution of Washington*, Publ. 477. Washington, 1937.

SHOOK, EDWIN M., and ALFRED V. KIDDER. 'Mound E–III–3, Kaminaljuyú, Guatemala', *Carnegie Institution of Washington, Contributions to American Anthropology and History*, no. 53. Washington, 1952.

STIRLING, MATTHEW W. 'Stone monuments of southern Mexico', *Bureau of American Ethnology*, Bulletin 138. Washington, 1943. (Contains a description of the monuments at Izapa.)

WILLEY, GORDON R. and JAMES C. GIFFORD. 'Pottery of the Holmul I style from Barton Ramie, British Honduras', in *Essays in Pre-Columbian Art and Archaeology* by Samuel K. Lothrop and others. 152–70. Cambridge, Mass., 1961.

CHAPTERS 4 AND 5

There are a great many publications on the Classic Maya civilization. Only a few of the most relevant can be listed here.

General Survey

PROSKOURIAKOFF, TATIANA. 'A study of Classic Maya art', *Carnegie Institution of Washington*, Publ. 593. Washington, 1950.

The Southern Maya Area

BORHEGYI, STEPHAN F. 'Aqualung archeology', *Natural History*, vol. LXVII, no. 3, 120–5. New York, 1958. (Describes underwater finds in Lake Amatitlán.)

KIDDER, ALFRED V., JESSE L. JENNINGS, and EDWIN M. SHOOK. 'Excavations at Kaminaljuyú, Guatemala', *Carnegie Institution of Washington*, Publ. 561. Washington, 1946.

SMITH, A. LEDYARD, and ALFRED V. KIDDER. 'Excavations at Nebaj, Guatemala', *Carnegie Institution of Washington*, Publ. 594. Washington, 1951.

THOMPSON, J. ERIC S. 'An archaeological reconnaissance in the Cotzumalhuapa region, Escuintla, Guatemala', *Carnegie Institution of Washington, Contributions to American Anthropology and History*, no. 44. Washington, 1948.

WAUCHOPE, ROBERT. 'Excavations at Zacualpa, Guatemala', *Middle American Research Institute*, Publ. no. 14. New Orleans, 1948.

The Central Maya Area

BULLARD, WILLIAM R., Jr. 'Maya settlement pattern in northeastern Petén, Guatemala', *American Antiquity*, vol. 25, no. 3, 355–72. Salt Lake City, 1960.

CARR, ROBERT F., and JAMES E. HAZARD. 'Map of the ruins of Tikal, El Petén, Guatemala', *Tikal Reports*, no. 11. Philadelphia, 1961.

COE, WILLIAM R. *Piedras Negras Archaeology: Artifacts, Caches, and Burials*. Philadelphia, 1959.

—, 'Tikal: ten years of study of a Maya ruin in the lowlands of Guatemala', *Expedition*, vol. 8, no. 1, 5–56. Philadelphia, 1965.

GORDON, GEORGE B. 'Prehistoric ruins of Copan, Honduras', *Memoirs of the Peabody Museum of Archaeology and Ethnology, Harvard University*, vol. 1, no. 1. Cambridge, 1896.

KIDDER, ALFRED V. 'The artifacts of Uaxactun, Guatemala', *Carnegie Institution of Washington*, Publ. 576. Washington, 1947.

LONGYEAR, JOHN M. 'Copan ceramics', *Carnegie Institution of Washington*, Publ. 597. Washington, 1952.

MALER, TEOBERT. 'Researches in the central portion of the Usumatsintla Valley'. *Memoirs of the Peabody Museum of Archaeology and Ethnology, Harvard University*, vol. 2, (no. 1, 1901; no. 2, 1903). Cambridge.

—, 'Explorations in the Department of Petén, Guatemala', *Memoirs of the Peabody Museum of Archaeology and Ethnology, Harvard University*, vol. 5, no. 1. Cambridge, 1911.

MORLEY, SYLVANUS G. 'The inscriptions of Copan', *Carnegie Institution of Washington*, Publ. 219. Washington, 1920.

—, 'Guide book to the ruins of Quiriguá', *Carnegie Institution of Washington*, Supplementary publ. 16. Washington, 1935.

—, 'The inscriptions of Petén', *Carnegie Institution of Washington*, Publ. 437. 5 vols. Washington, 1937–8.

RUPPERT, KARL, J. ERIC S. THOMPSON, and TATIANA PROSKOURIAKOFF, 'Bonampak, Chiapas, Mexico', *Carnegie Institution of Washington*, Publ. 602. Washington, 1955.

RUZ, ALBERTO. 'Exploraciones en Palenque', in *Proceedings of the Thirtieth International Congress of Americanists*, 5–22. Cambridge, 1954.

—, 'Palenque', *Official Guide, Instituto Nacional de Antropología e Historia*. Mexico, 1960.

SMITH, A. LEDYARD. 'Uaxactun, Guatemala: excavations of 1931–7', *Carnegie Institution of Washington*, Publ. 588. Washington, 1950.

SMITH, ROBERT E. 'Ceramic sequence at Uaxactun, Guatemala' (see under chapter 2).

STROMSVIK, GUSTAV. 'Guide book to the ruins of Copan', *Carnegie Institution of Washington*, Publ. 577. Washington, 1947.

THOMPSON, J. ERIC S. 'Excavations at San Jose, British Honduras', *Carnegie Institution of Washington*, Publ. 506. Washington, 1939.

TOZZER, ALFRED M. 'A preliminary study of the prehistoric ruins of Tikal, Guatemala', *Memoirs of the Peabody Museum of Archaeology and Ethnology, Harvard University*, vol. 5, no. 2. Cambridge, 1911.

WILLEY, GORDON R. 'The structure of ancient Maya society: evidence from the southern lowlands', *American Anthropologist*, vol. 58, no. 5, 777–82. Menasha, 1956.

WILLEY, GORDON R., *et al.* 'Prehistoric Maya settlements in the Belize Valley', *Papers of the Peabody Museum of Archaeology and Ethnology, Harvard University*, vol. 54. Cambridge, 1965.

The Northern Maya Area

ANDREWS, E. WYLLYS. 'Excavations at Dzibilchaltún, northwestern Yucatan, Mexico', *Proceedings of the American Philosophical Society*, vol. 104, no. 3, 254–65. Philadelphia, 1960.

BRAINERD, GEORGE W. 'The archaeological ceramics of Yucatan' (see under chapter 2).

GROTH-KIMBALL, IRMGARD. *Maya Terrakotten*. Tübingen, 1960. (Excellent photographs of Jaina figurines.)

RUPPERT, KARL, and J. H. DENNISON Jr. 'Archaeological Reconnaissance in Campeche, Quintana Roo, and Petén', *Carnegie Institution of Washington*, Publ. 543. Washington, 1943.

RUZ, ALBERTO. *Campeche en la Arqueologia Maya*. Mexico, 1945.

—, 'Uxmal', *Guía Oficial, Instituto Nacional de Antropología e Historia*, Mexico, 1956.

STEPHENS, JOHN L. *Incidents of Travel in Yucatan* (see under chapter 1; still the best guide to the Puuc sites).

Thompson, J. Eric S., *et al.* 'A preliminary study of the ruins of Cobá, Quintana Roo, Mexico', *Carnegie Institution of Washington*, Publ. 424. Washington, 1932.

CHAPTER 6

Barrera Vásquez, Alfredo, and Sylvanus G. Morley. 'The Maya chronicles', *Carnegie Institution of Washington, Contributions to American Anthropology and History*, no. 48. Washington, 1949.

Brinton, Daniel G. *The Maya Chronicles.* Philadelphia, 1882.

Chamberlain, Robert S. 'The conquest and colonization of Yucatan', *Carnegie Institution of Washington*, Publ. 582. Washington, 1948.

Gann, Thomas. 'Mounds in northern Honduras', *Bureau of American Ethnology, 19th Annual Report*, part 2, 655–92. Washington, 1900 (illustrates the Santa Rita frescoes).

Lothrop, Samuel K. 'Tulum, an archaeological study of the east coast of Yucatan', *Carnegie Institution of Washington*, Publ. 335. Washington, 1924.

—, 'Metals from the Cenote of Sacrifice, Chichen Itzá, Yucatan', *Memoirs of the Peabody Museum of Archaeology and Ethnology, Harvard University*, vol. 10, no. 2. Cambridge, 1952.

Morris, Earl H., *et al.* 'The temple of the Warriors at Chichen Itzá, Yucatan', *Carnegie Institution of Washington*, Publ. 406. 2 vols. Washington, 1931.

Pollock, H. E. D., *et al.* 'Mayapan, Yucatan, Mexico'. *Carnegie Institution of Washington*, Publ. 619. Washington, 1962. (The account of Itzá history in chapter 6 is based upon the Roys essay.)

Recinos, Adrian. *Popol Vuh: the Sacred Book of the Ancient Quiché Maya.* Norman, Oklahoma, 1950.

Recinos, Adrian, and Delia Goetz. *The Annals of the Cakchiquels.* Norman, Oklahoma, 1953.

Roys, Ralph L. 'The Book of Chilam Balam of Chumayel', *Carnegie Institution of Washington*, Publ. 438. Washington, 1933.

—, 'The political geography of the Yucatan Maya', *Carnegie Institution of Washington*, Publ. 613. Washington, 1957.

RUPPERT, KARL. 'The Caracol at Chichen Itzá, Yucatan, Mexico', *Carnegie Institution of Washington*, Publ. 454. Washington, 1935.

SANDERS, WILLIAM T. 'Prehistoric ceramics and settlement patterns in Quintana Roo, Mexico', *Carnegie Institution of Washington*, Publ. 606, 155–264. Washington, 1960.

SHEPARD, ANNA O. 'Plumbate, a Mesoamerican trade ware', *Carnegie Institution of Washington*, Publ. 573. Washington, 1948.

SMITH, A. LEDYARD. 'Archaeological reconnaissance in central Guatemala', *Carnegie Institution of Washington*, Publ. 608. Washington, 1955.

THOMPSON, J. ERIC S. 'A co-ordination of the history of Chichen Itzá with ceramic sequences in central Mexico', *Revista Mexicana de Estudios Antropológicos*, vol. 5, 97–111. Mexico, 1941.

TOZZER, ALFRED M. 'Chichen Itzá and its Cenote of Sacrifice', *Memoirs of the Peabody Museum of Archaeology and Ethnology, Harvard University*, vols. 11, 12. Cambridge, 1957.

WOODBURY, RICHARD B., and TRIK, AUBREY. *The Ruins of Zaculeu, Guatemala*. 2 vols. Boston, 1953.

CHAPTER 7

BLOM, FRANS. 'Commerce, trade, and monetary units of the Maya', *Middle American Research Series*, no. 4, 557–66. New Orleans, 1932.

COE, MICHAEL D. 'A model of ancient community structure in the Maya Lowlands', *Southwestern Journal of Anthropology*, vol. 21, no. 2, 97–114. Albuquerque, 1965.

EDMUNDSON, MUNRO S. 'Historia de las tierras altas mayas, según los documentos indígenas', in *Desarrollo Cultural de los Mayas*, Vogt and Ruz (eds.), 255–78 (see under chapter 1).

FOLLETT, PRESCOTT, H. F. 'War and weapons of the Maya', *Middle American Research Series*, Publ. 4, 374–410. New Orleans, 1932.

MILES, S. W. 'The sixteenth-century Pokom-Maya: a documentary analysis of social structure and archaeological setting', *Transactions of the American Philosophical Society*, vol. 47, part 4. Philadelphia, 1957.

ROYS, RALPH L. 'The Indian background of Colonial Yucatan', *Carnegie Institution of Washington*, Publ. 548. Washington, 1943.

SCHOLES, FRANCE V. and RALPH L. ROYS. 'The Maya Chontal Indians of Acalan-Tixchel', *Carnegie Institution of Washington*, Publ. 560. Washington, 1948.

THOMPSON, J. ERIC S. 'Trade relations between the Maya highlands and lowlands', *Estudios de Cultura Maya*, vol. IV, 13–49. Mexico, 1964.

TOZZER, ALFRED M. 'Landa's Relación de las Cosas de Yucatán' (see under chapter 1; this is the most important work on Maya life in the late pre-Conquest period).

CHAPTER 8

ANDERS, FERDINAND. *Das Pantheon der Maya*. Graz, Austria, 1963.

BERLIN, HEINRICH. 'El glifo "emblema" en las inscripciones mayas', *Journal de la Société des Américanistes*, vol. 47, 111–19. Paris, 1958.

KELLEY, DAVID H. 'A history of the decipherment of Maya script', *Anthropological Linguistics*, vol. 4, no. 8. Bloomington, Indiana, 1962.

—, 'Fonetismo en la escritura maya', *Estudios de Cultura Maya*, vol. II, 277–318. Mexico, 1962.

—, 'Glyphic evidence for a dynastic sequence at Quiriguá, Guatemala', *American Antiquity*, vol. 27, 323–5. Salt Lake City, 1962.

KNOROSOV, YURI V. 'The problem of the study of the Maya hieroglyphic writing', *American Antiquity*, vol. 23, no 3, 284–91. Salt Lake City, 1958.

—, *Pis'mennost' Indeitsev Maiia* (Writing of the Maya Indians). Moscow-Leningrad, 1963.

MORLEY, SYLVANUS G. 'An introduction to the study of the Maya hieroglyphs', *Bureau of American Ethnology*, Bulletin 57. Washington, 1915.

PROSKOURIAKOFF, TATIANA. 'Historical implications of a pattern of dates at Piedras Negras, Guatemala', *American Antiquity*, vol. 25, no. 4, 454–75. Salt Lake City, 1960. (A now classic paper.)

—, 'The lords of the Maya realm', *Expedition*, vol. 4, no. 1, 14–21. Philadelphia, 1961.

—, 'Portraits of women in Maya art', in *Essays in Pre-Columbian Art and Archaeology*, S. K. Lothrop and others, 81–99. Cambridge, 1961.

SÁNCHEZ, GEORGE I. *Arithmetic in Maya*. Austin, Texas, 1961.

SATTERTHWAITE, LINTON, Jr. 'Concepts and structures of Maya calendrical arithmetics', *Joint Publications of the Museum of the University of Pennsylvania and the Philadelphia Anthropological Society*, no. 3. Philadelphia, 1947.

TEEPLE, JOHN E. 'Maya astronomy', *Carnegie Institution of Washington, Contributions to American Archaeology*, no. 2. Washington, 1930.

THOMPSON, J. ERIC S. 'Maya arithmetic', *Carnegie Institution of Washington, Contributions to American Anthropology and History*, no. 36. Washington, 1942.

—, 'Maya hieroglyphic writing. Introduction', *Carnegie Institution of Washington*, Publ. 589. Washington, 1950. (A monumental survey of Maya calendrics, religion, and astronomy.)

—, *A Catalogue of Maya Hieroglyphs*. Norman, Oklahoma, 1962. (Covers glyphs of both the monuments and codices.)

VILLACORTA, J. ANTONIO and CARLOS A. *Códices mayas*. Guatemala, 1930 (All three Maya hieroglyphic books reproduced in a useful edition.)

ZIMMERMAN, GÜNTER. *Die Hieroglyphen der Maya-Handschriften*. Hamburg, 1956. (A catalogue of the glyphs in the codices.)

Sources of Illustrations

Grateful acknowledgement is made to the following persons and institutions who have kindly provided photographs and permission to publish them:

American Museum of Natural History, New York, 1, 33–5, 47, 57, 58, 62 (Erickson Collection), 74; Stephan F. Borhegyi and the Milwaukee Public Museum, 29; Frederick Church Collection, Olana, New York, 3; Dumbarton Oaks, Washington, D.C., 50, 60, 63, 66, 68; Ian Graham, 61; Museum of Primitive Art, New York, 21–3, 25 (photographs by Charles Uht); Museum für Völkerkunde, Basel, 38; Lee A. Parsons, 6; Peabody Museum, Harvard University, 2, 5, 8–11, 14–16, 24, 26–8, 30, 31, 36, 42–4, 52–4, 69, 73, 75–8, 80–82; Alberto Ruz L., 48–50; Trustees of the British Museum, 40, 65, 67; University Museum, Philadelphia, 12, 13, 17–20, 37, 41; Charles R. Wicke, 70, 72.

Figures 1–3, 6–7, 13, 15, 18, 28, 33 were drawn by Mrs Jean Zallinger and Mr Peter Zallinger, and Figures 5, 8–10, 12, 34, 35, 40, 43–5, 48–50 by the author. Others were reproduced from various publications. Sources for both drawings and reproductions are as follows: Figure 6, E. M. Shook, 'The present status of research'; Figure 13, 'Mound E–III–3, Kaminaljuyú, Guatemala'; Figure 14, R. Girard, *Los Mayas Eternos* (figure 242); Figure 16, A. V. Kidder, J. Jennings and E. M. Shook, 'Excavations at Kaminaljuyú, Guatemala' (figure 108); Figure 17, F. R. and S. G. Morley, 'The age and provenance of the Leyden Plate'; Figure 18, R. E. Smith, 'Ceramic sequence at Uaxactún, Guatemala'; Figure 19, H. Moholy-Nagy, 'A Tlaloc stela from Tikal'; Figure 21, R. F. Carr and J. E. Hazard, 'Map of the ruins of Tikal'; Figures 23–4, 39, A. Trik, 'The splendid tomb of Temple I, Tikal, Guatemala'; Figure 25, W. H. Holmes, *Archaeological Studies among the Ancient Cities of Mexico* (figure 64); Figure 26, A. Ruz L., 'Exploraciones en Palenque: 1951' (figure 5); Figure 27, George Kubler, *The Art and Architecture of Ancient America* (figure 47), courtesy Professor Kubler; Figure 29, Carnegie Institution of Washington, 'The Art of the Maya'; Figure 30, 31, S. K. Lothrop, 'Metals from the Cenote of Sacrifice'; Figure 34, S. K. Lothrop, 'Tulum' (plate 25); Figures 36–7, T. A. Joyce, 'The pottery whistle-figurines of Lubaantun'; Figure 38, H. T. Webster, 'Tikal graffiti' (figure 12); Figure 41, G. Zimmermann, *Die Hieroglyphen der Maya-Handschriften* (tables 6, 7); Figure 42, T. A. Joyce, *Mexican Archaeology* (figure 58); Figure 46, E. J. Palacios, 'Inscripción recientemente descubierta en Palenque' (figure 1); Figure 51, T. Proskouriakoff, 'Historical data in the inscriptions of Yaxchilan' (figure 1).

Notes on the Plates

1 The Lacandón rain forest, Chiapas, Mexico, from photograph by Dr T. C. Schneirla.

2 Lake Atitlán in the Maya highlands, Guatemala. This view was taken in the 1880s and shows native traders carrying loads of pottery to market.

3 Burning a lowland *milpa* at Uaxactún, Petén, Guatemala.

4 Pottery figurine of a seated woman, Copolchí, Guatemala. Height *c.* 4 in. Las Charcas culture, Middle Formative Period.

5 Fluted point of obsidian, San Rafael, Guatemala. Length 5.7 cm. Early Hunters Period.

6 Monument 1, Monte Alto, Guatemala. Height 4 ft 8 in. Probably Late Formative Period.

7 Effigy bowl of grey-green chlorite schist from Tomb 1, Mound E–III–3, Kaminaljuyú, Guatemala. Over-all length 21 cm. Miraflores culture, Late Formative Period.

8 North side of Pyramid E–VII–sub, Uaxactún, Guatemala. Height 8 m. Chicanel culture, Late Formative Period. On top of this stucco-faced pyramid had once been a pole-and-thatch temple.

9 Fine-line incised bowl from Tomb I, Mound E–III–3, Kaminaljuyú, Guatemala. Width 30.5 cm. Miraflores culture, Late Formative Period.

10 Grey soapstone jar from Tomb I, Mound E–III–3, Kaminaljuyú, Guatemala. Height 9.2 cm. Miraflores culture, Late Formative Period.

11 Granite stela of a man wearing masks of the Long-lipped God, Kaminaljuyú, Guatemala. Height 6 ft. Miraflores culture, Late Formative Period.

12 Green stone mask, with shell-inlaid teeth and eyes, from Burial 85, Tikal, Guatemala. Height 5 in. Chicanel culture, Late Formative Period.

13 Tripod vessel with cover, from Tomb B–II, Kaminaljuyú, Guatemala. Height 32 cm. Esperanza culture, Early Classic Period. The exterior had been stuccoed and painted in buff, red, and light green. The figures on the vessel are Maya, while the glyphs on the lid are Teotihuacanoid.

14 Usulután ware bowl from Burial 85, Tikal, Guatemala. Diameter c. 20 cm. Chicanel culture, Late Formative Period.

15 Restored Thin Orange ware vessel in the form of a seated man, from Tomb X, Kaminaljuyú, Guatemala. Height of vessel c. 30 cm. Esperanza culture, Early Classic Period. This ware was manufactured to Teotihuacán taste in northern Puebla, and appears wherever the Teotihuacán people had penetrated.

16 Lid of stuccoed bowl from Burial 10, Tikal. The head and hands painted here in Teotihuacán style belong to Xipe Totec, the Mexican god of the springtime. Tzakol culture, Early Classic Period.

17 The tomb chamber of Burial 48, Tikal, Guatemala. On its walls is painted the Long Count date 9.1.1.10.10 4 Oc (18 March, A.D. 457), along with other glyphs of probably stellar significance. Tzakol culture, Early Classic Period.

18 Long jade bead carved with human figure, from Tomb A–VI, Kaminaljuyú, Guatemala. Length 15.6 cm. Esperanza culture, Early Classic Period.

19 Side view of Stela 31, Tikal, with relief figure of a warrior in Teotihuacán costume. In one hand he carries an *atlatl* or spear-thrower, and in the other, a shield with the face of Tlaloc, the Mexican Rain God. Tzakol culture, Early Classic Period.

20, 21 Seated figure of wood, from unknown site in Tabasco, Mexico. Height 14 in. This, the finest Maya wood carving known, represents a moustachioed lord with folded arms; traces of hematite pigment remain on the piece. Tzakol culture, Early Classic Period.

22 Polychrome two-part effigy of pottery from Burial 10, Tikal, Guatemala. Height 36 cm. This may represent the supreme god Itzamná receiving a severed head as an offering. Tzakol culture, Early Classic Period.

23 Double chambered vessel, possibly from Campeche, Mexico. Height 11⅞ in. On the two lids a young man faces a fantastic bird. Tzakol culture, Early Classic Period.

24 Jade plaque of the Rain God, Copán, Honduras. Height 4¼ in. Early Classic Period.

25 Jade object shaped like an ear flare, Pomona, British Honduras. Diameter 7 in. The four glyphs probably refer to gods. Tzakol culture, Early Classic Period.

26 Stone relief of Crab God, El Baúl, Guatemala. Height 1 m. On either side are the Mexican dates 2 Monkey and 6 Monkey. Cotzumalhuapa culture, end of Early Classic or beginning of Late Classic Period.

27 Part of upper façade of building, Acanceh, Mexico. The stuccoed figures are in Teotihuacán style. Shown here is a jaguar or puma, a speech scroll issuing from its mouth. Early Classic Period.

28 Thin stone head (*hacha*) from El Baúl, Guatemala. Height *c*. 1 ft. Objects of this sort were probably ball court markers. Cotzumalhuapa culture, end of Early Classic or beginning of Late Classic Period.

29 Pottery incense burner with heads of the Death God and Xipe Totec, Mexican god of the springtime, from the Zarzal underwater site, Lake Amatitlán, Guatemala. Height 24 cm. Early Classic Period.

30 Restoration drawing of the site of Copán, Honduras, by Tatiana Proskouriakoff. To the right is the Acropolis, to the left the Great Plaza. The bulk of the construction shown here is of the Late Classic Period.

31 Ball Court, Copán, Honduras, from the south. Late Classic Period.

32 Stone head and torso of the Young Maize God, Copán, Honduras. Height 28 in. Late Classic Period.

33 Head of torchbearer on the Reviewing Stand, Copán, Honduras, from photograph by Dr Gordon Ekholm. Approximately life-sized. Late Classic Period. This grotesque sculpture is very reminiscent of the Cotzumalhuapa style.

34 Stela D and its 'altar', north side of the Great Plaza, Copán, Honduras, from a lithograph published by Frederick Catherwood in 1844. Height of stela, 11 ft 9 in. The 'altar' represents the Death God with fleshless jaws. On the stela is the *tun* ending date 9.15.5.0.0 (26 July, A.D. 736). Late Classic Period.

35 Altar of Zoomorph O, Quiriguá, Guatemala. Length 12 ft 4 in. On the left of this enormous monument, which was dedicated on the *katun* ending 9.18.0.0.0 (11 October, A.D. 790), is a figure of a masked dancer in the coils of a serpent. Late Classic Period.

36 Stela D, Quiriguá, Guatemala, from photograph taken by A. P. Maudslay in 1885. Height 19 ft 6 in. This monument was erected on 9.16.15.0.0, or 19 February, A.D. 766. Late Classic Period.

37 Temple I, Tikal, Guatemala. Total height 155 ft. The stelae in the foreground are arranged before the terrace of the North Acropolis. Late Classic Period.

38 Room in the Five-Story Palace, Tikal, Guatemala, from photograph taken by Teobert Maler. The use to which these 'palaces' were put remains uncertain. As seen here, there are usually one or more plastered benches along the back wall of the rooms. Late Classic Period.

39 Lintel 24 from Structure 23, Yaxchilán, Guatemala. Height 3 ft 7 in. A richly robed woman kneels before the Yaxchilán ruler 'Shield Jaguar', and draws blood by passing a rope with thorns through her tongue. This relief was dedicated in A.D. 709, not long after 'Shield Jaguar' had captured his enemy 'Death'. Late Classic Period.

40 Carved wooden lintel from Temple IV, Tikal, Guatemala. Length in greatest dimension 6 ft 9 in. Beneath the body of a double-headed feathered serpent is seated a Maya lord upon a throne, with spear in one hand and shield in the other. The terraced platform below is apparently a sort of palanquin. Probably dedicated in A.D. 747, Late Classic Period.

41 Sculptured Stone 1, Bonampak, Mexico. A Maya lord is seated on a dais above three lesser figures. First half of seventh century A.D., Late Classic Period.

42 Detail of wall painting in Room 1, Bonampak, Mexico. Musicians sing and beat time, while to the left performs a group of mummers masked as water gods. About A.D. 800, Late Classic Period.

43 Wall painting in Room 2, Bonampak, Mexico. On a terraced platform stands the ruler of Bonampak and his subordinates. Below, captives taken in a jungle skirmish are being tortured by having their finger-nails removed. About A.D. 800, Late Classic Period.

44 Stela 14, Piedras Negras, Guatemala. Height 9 ft 3 in. The monument marks the accession to the throne in A.D. 761 of the young lord seated in the niche. At the foot of the platform stands a middle-aged woman, perhaps the new king's mother. Late Classic Period.

45 Decorated pier on the Palace, Palenque, Mexico, from a photograph by A. P. Maudslay. In this stucco relief, both figures grasp a fantastic serpent. Late Classic Period.

46 Temple of the Sun, Palenque, Mexico, from the north-east. Early eighth century A.D. Late Classic Period.

47 Life-sized jade mosaic mask from the Funerary Crypt, Temple of the Inscriptions, Palenque, Mexico. The eyes were fashioned of shell and obsidian, and all the pieces were affixed to a wooden backing, now rotted away. Late seventh or early eighth century A.D., Late Classic Period.

48 Detail from Panel of the Slaves, Palenque, Mexico. Shown here is the head of the principal figure, who sits cross-legged on the back of two crouching captives. On either side of him are placed a man and woman carrying offerings in their hands. Eighth century A.D., Late Classic Period.

49 The Palace and Tower from the south-west, Palenque, Mexico. Late Classic Period. In the distance is the flood plain of the Rió Usumacinta.

50 East wing of the Nunnery, Chichen Itzá, Mexico, from a lithograph by Frederick Catherwood. The masks repeated so many times on this kind of façade are believed to be of the sky-serpent. Puuc culture, end of the Late Classic Period.

51 Funerary Crypt in the Temple of the Inscriptions, Palenque, Mexico. The sarcophagus lies below and supports the great stone slab. Around the walls of the corbelled chamber are nine stuccoed figures. Late seventh or early eighth century A.D., Late Classic Period

52 North façade of Structure V, Hormiguero, Mexico, from a photograph taken by Karl Ruppert in 1933. The figure stands before the doorway of the one-room temple, entered through the jaws of a monstrous mask. On the west side are the remains of a false tower. Río Bec culture, end of the Late Classic Period.

53 Palace at Xpuhil, from a reconstruction drawing by Tatiana Proskouriakoff. The three towers are completely solid and served

no other function than decoration. Río Bec culture, end of the Late Classic Period.

54 Arch at Labná, Mexico, from a view published by Frederick Catherwood in 1844. Puuc culture, end of the Late Classic Period.

55 West wing of Palace, Sayil, Mexico. Seemingly three-storied, each row of rooms actually rests on a solid rubble core. The vaults have collapsed in the lower 'storey'. Puuc culture, end of the Late Classic Period.

56 Stone lintel from Kuná (Lacanhá), Mexico. Height 27¼ in. A seated male figure holds a 'ceremonial bar', a stylized, double-headed sky-serpent. In the text to the left is carved the *tun* ending 9.15.15.0.0 (4 June, A.D. 746). Late Classic Period.

57 Large pottery censer, probably from Tabasco, Mexico. Height 23¾ in. The main face is that of the Jaguar God of the Under-world, the guise of the Sun on his nightly journey beneath the earth. Censers of this form were especially popular at Palenque. Late Classic Period.

58 Pottery figurine of a woman sheltering a man, Jaina, Mexico. Height 8 in. Late Classic Period.

59 Pottery figurine, probably from Jaina, Mexico. Height 11½ in. The subject is the Fat God, wearing feathered war costume and carrying a shield. Late Classic Period.

60 Pottery figurine, Jaina, Mexico. Height 8½ in. A seated man holds an unidentified object, possibly a celt. Like all of the finest pieces from Jaina, this figurine was made partly with a pottery mould and partly with the fingers, and was painted after firing. Late Classic Period.

61 Incised pottery bowl, slateware, from the Northern Area. Height 4½ in. The design, a modified step-and-fret pattern, is carried out in a negative smudging technique. Late Classic Period.

62 Onyx marble bowl, said to be from the state of Campeche, Mexico. Height 4½ in. A row of incised glyphs encircles the rim. Below, on the fluted sides, are incised three seated profile figures, two men and a robed woman, with additional glyphs; each figure holds a symbolic object. Late Classic Period.

63 Black pottery jar, from Chocholá (southern Yucatán), Mexico. Height 5½ in. The vessel has been deeply carved with the figure of the Sun God against a swirling background, and red pigment rubbed into the cut-away areas. Late Classic Period.

64 Polychrome pottery vase from Altar de Sacrificios, Guatemala. Height 10 in. This side shows an old man, perhaps the God Itzamná, apparently dead, but dancing with a monstrous snake. Five other figures appear on the vase, all with death associations. In the text is a Calendar Round date probably corresponding to A.D. 754. Tepeu culture, Late Classic Period.

65 Incised obsidians from a stela cache, Tikal, Guatemala. Length of longest piece 2¾ in. The flat side of a crude flake has in each instance been engraved with the figure of a deity or with a simplified mat design. Tepeu culture, Late Classic Period.

66 Carved jade plaque, Nebaj, Guatemala. Width 5¾ in. This piece is emerald green with white clouding, and represents a Maya lord in conversation with a dwarf. Late Classic Period.

67 Eccentric flint from Group A, Quiriguá, Guatemala. Length 10 in. Two human profiles can be seen facing left in a tour-de-force of the flint chipper's art. Tepeu culture. Late Classic Period.

68 Carved shell pendant, probably from Jaina, Mexico. Height 3⅛ in. A young man with the flattened head so highly esteemed by the Maya appears above a fantastic fish, the body of which is covered with unreadable glyphs. The cut-away areas were once inlaid with jade. Late Classic Period.

69 View of the Toltec part of Chichen Itzá, Mexico, looking north-east from the Nunnery. In the foreground is the Caracol; beyond it to the left, the Castillo or Temple of Kukulcan; and to the right, the Temple of the Warriors. Toltec-Maya culture, Early Post-Classic Period.

70 Chacmool at head of stairs, Temple of the Warriors, Chichen Itzá, Mexico. Height 3 ft 6 in. Reclining figures of this sort were introduced by the Toltec, and are thought to be connected with the cult of heart sacrifice. Toltec-Maya culture, Early Post-Classic Period.

71 The Temple of the Warriors from a doorway of the Castillo, Chichen Itzá, Mexico. The building is a grandiose replica of Pyramid B at Tula, in Mexico, and a symbol of Toltec ascendancy over Yucatán. Toltec-Maya culture, Early Post-Classic Period.

72 Ball Court, Chichen Itzá, Mexico, with walls 27 feet high, and with an over-all length of about 490 feet, this is the largest court in Mesoamerica. The rings set high on either wall were used in scoring the game. Toltec-Maya culture, Early Post-Classic Period.

73 Doorway of the Temple of the Tigers, overlooking the Ball Court, Chichen Itzá, Mexico. Shown here are one of two Feathered Serpent columns which support the lintel, and a door jamb with a relief figure of a Toltec warrior. Toltec-Maya culture, Early Post-Classic Period.

74 Upper part of pottery incense burner, Mayapán, Mexico. Height 9½ in. God M, Ek Chuah, who was the patron of merchants, is shown here, identifiable from his partly broken, Pinocchio-like nose. Red, blue, and yellow paint had been applied to the censer. Mayapán culture, Middle Post-Classic Period.

75 Relief panel of a jaguar eating a heart, from the Dance Platform of the Eagles, Chichen Itzá, Mexico. Such a theme is also known at Tula in the Toltec homeland, and is symbolic of the military order of the Jaguars. Toltec-Maya culture, Early Post-Classic Period.

76 X-Fine Orange ware jar, from coastal Campeche, Mexico. Height c. 7 in. Along with Plumbate ware, pottery of this kind is a marker for the Toltec presence in the Maya area. The vessel shown has a design of hands in black paint. Toltec-Maya culture, Early Post-Classic Period.

77 Tripod jar, Plumbate ware, from coastal Campeche, Mexico. Height 7½ in. Produced on the Pacific slopes of Chiapas and Guatemala in Toltec style, this glazed ware was widely traded over much of southern Mesoamerica. Toltec-Maya culture, Early Post-Classic Period.

78 Effigy jar, Plumbate ware, in the form of a bearded old man, from Guatemala. Height 6 in. Toltec-Maya culture, Early Post-Classic Period.

79 Temple of the Frescoes, Tulum, Mexico, from the west; the photograph was taken prior to 1923 by a Carnegie Institution of Washington expedition, before the walled site had been cleared. The temple, which lies at the centre of Tulum, is noted for its wall paintings carried out in a hybrid Mixtec-Maya style. Inset panels over the doorways contain stucco 'diving god' figures, while stuccoed faces at the corners of the lower storey suggest its dedication to the god Itzamná. Middle to Late Post-Classic Period.

80 Group B, Mixco Viejo, Guatemala, looking east. The ruins of the Pokomam capital are surrounded on all sides by tremendously precipitous ravines. To take the town from its defenders, Alvarado's army had to advance up a steep path along which only two abreast could move, under a hail of rocks and poisoned arrows. This is the main group of the site, dominated by the usual double temple. Middle to Late Post-Classic Period.

81 Group C, Chuitinamit, Guatemala, looking west; restoration drawing by Tatiana Proskouriakoff. The Quiché built an impressive stronghold here after driving out the Pokomam Maya. A typically Mexican feature of the late highland centres is the double pyramid in the middle of the group. In the background can be seen a ball court. Middle to Late Post-Classic Period.

82 Pottery incense burner from shrine at Mayapán, Mexico. Height 21½ in. This effigy of God B, the Rain God Chac, carries a small bowl in one hand and a ball of flaming incense in the other. The censer was painted after firing with blue, green, black, red, white, and yellow pigments. Mayapán culture, Middle Post-Classic Period.

83 Page from the Dresden Codex. Height 8 in. The most beautiful and the earliest of the three surviving folding-screen books of the Maya, the Dresden was written on a long strip of bark paper, each page coated with fine stucco. Much of the codex, as in the case of the page shown here, is concerned with 260-day ritual counts divided up in various ways, the divisions being associated with specific gods. The texts immediately above each deity contain their names and epithets. Early Post-Classic Period.

Index

More About Penguins
and Pelicans

Other Pelicans of interest